ADAM ZAGAJEWSKI was born in Lvov in 1945. His books in English include *Tremor* (1985), *Canvas* (1991), and *Mysticism for Beginners* (1997), collections of poetry; and *Solidarity, Solitude* (1990), *Two Cities* (1995), and *Another Beauty* (2000), collections of essays. He lives in Paris and Houston.

CLARE CAVANAGH is a professor of Slavic languages at Northwestern University, and has also translated the poetry of Wyslawa Szymborska.

RENATA GORCZYNSKI is an essayist, a literary critic, and a teacher of journalism. She lives in Gdynia, Poland.

BENJAMIN IVRY is a poet ("Paradise for the Portuguese Queen"), biographer (of Ravel, Poulenc, and Rimbaud), and translator. He is working on a life of Olivier Messiaen.

C. K. WILLIAMS's awards for poetry include the National Book Critics Circle Award and the Pulitzer Prize. He teaches at Princeton University.

WITHOUT END

gift
Dr. m dS

WITHOUT END

NEW AND SELECTED POEMS

ADAM ZAGAJEWSKI

TRANSLATED BY CLARE CAVANAGH

AND RENATA GORCZYNSKI, BENJAMIN IVRY,

AND C. K. WILLIAMS

FARRAR, STRAUS AND GIROUX

NEW YORK

Farrar, Straus and Giroux
19 Union Square West, New York 10003

Grateful acknowledgment is made to the following publications, in which
some of these poems first appeared: *Agni* ("Smoke" and "The Soul"); *Chicago
Review* ("Where the Breath Is," "Escalator," and "Dead Sparrow"); *Double-
take* ("Separation" and "The World's Prose"); *Euphony* ("Europe Goes to
Sleep" and "Stary Sacz"); *Gulf Coast* ("December"); *Literary Imagination*
("Ancient History," "Senza Flash," and "Little Waltz"); *New England Review*
("Vaporetto" and "How Clowns Go"); *The New Republic* ("A Flame," "Eu-
rope Goes to Sleep," "Barbarians," "Lindens," "Death of a Pianist," "Square
d'Orléans," and "A Morning in Vicenza"); *The New Yorker* ("Just Children,"
"Try to Praise the Mutilated World," "The Early Hours," and "Summer's
Fullness"); *The New York Review of Books* ("Farewell for Zbigniew Her-
bert," "My Aunts," "Europe in Winter," "Opus Posthumous," "To See," and
"How High the Moon"); *Partisan Review* ("Circus," "Castle," and "Speak
Softly"); and *Tin House* ("Little Waltz").

The Library of Congress has cataloged the hardcover edition as follows:
Zagajewski, Adam, 1945–
    [Poems. English. Selections]
    Without end : new and selected poems / Adam Zagajewski ; translations
by Clare Cavanagh . . . [et al.].
        p.   cm.
    Translated from Polish.
    ISBN-13: 978-0-374-22096-9
    ISBN-10: 0-374-22096-4 (hardcover : alk. paper)
    1. Zagajewski, Adam, 1945—Translations into English.   I. Cavanagh,
Clare.   II. Title.

PG7185.A32 A23 2002
891.8'5173—dc21

                                                                      2001040252

Paperback ISBN-13: 978-0-374-52861-4
Paperback ISBN-10: 0-374-52861-6

Designed by Jonathan D. Lippincott

www.fsgbooks.com

12   11   10   9   8   7   6   5

CONTENTS

EARLY POEMS (1970–1975) (translated by Clare Cavanagh)

FROM *MYSTICISM FOR BEGINNERS* (1997)
(translated by Clare Cavanagh)

NEW POEMS

TRANSLATED BY CLARE CAVANAGH

TO SEE

Oh my mute city, honey-gold,
buried in ravines, where wolves
loped softly down the cold meridian;
if I had to tell you, city,
asleep beneath a heap of lifeless leaves,
if I needed to describe the ocean's skin, on which
ships etch the lines of shining poems,
and yachts like peacocks flaunt their lofty sails
and the Mediterranean, rapt in salty concentration,
and cities with sharp turrets gleaming
in the keen morning sun,
and the savage strength of jets piercing the clouds,
the bureaucrats' undying scorn for us, people,
Umbria's narrow streets like cisterns
that stop up ancient time tasting of sweet wine,
and a certain hill, where the stillest tree is growing,
gray Paris, threaded by the river of salvation,
Krakow, on Sunday, when even chestnut leaves
seem pressed by an unseen iron,
vineyards raided by the greedy fall
and by highways full of fear;
if I had to describe the sobriety of the night
when it happened,
and the clatter of the train running into nothingness
and the blade flaring on a makeshift skating rink;
I'm writing from the road, I had to see,
and not just know, to see clearly
the sights and fires of a single world,
but you unmoving city turned to stone,
my brethren in the shallow sand;
the earth still turns above you

and the Roman legions march
and a polar fox attends the wind
in a white wasteland where sounds perish.

THE SOUL

We know we're not allowed to use your name.
We know you're inexpressible,
anemic, frail, and suspect
for mysterious offenses as a child.
We know that you are not allowed to live now
in music or in trees at sunset.
We know—or at least we've been told—
that you do not exist at all, anywhere.
And yet we still keep hearing your weary voice
—in an echo, a complaint, in the letters we receive
from Antigone in the Greek desert.

FAREWELL FOR ZBIGNIEW HERBERT

At first only cherries and the comic flight
of bats, the apple moon, a drowsy owl,
the tang of icy water on school outings.
The city's towers rise like words of love.
Afterwards, long after, Provence's golden dust,
fig trees in the vineyards, the lesson of white Greece,
obscure museums, Piero's Madonna great with child
—in the interim, two occupations, two inhuman armies,
death's clumsy vehicles patrol your streets.

Long days spent translating Georg Trakl,
"The Captive Blackbird's Song," that blissful first Paris
after years of Soviet scarcity and squalor;
your sly smile, your schoolboy jokes, the gravitas
and cheer you brought to Meaux's little cathedral
(Bossuet watched us rather dourly),
Berlin evenings: Herr Doktor, Herr Privatdozent,
the rice you scattered at friends' weddings like confetti—
but the quiet bitterness of bad months, too.

I liked to imagine your strolls
in Umbria, Liguria: your dapper chase,
your quest for places where the glaciers
of the past melt, baring forms.
I liked to imagine you roving
through poetry's mountains, seeking the spot
where silence suddenly erupts in speech.
But I always met you in the cramped apartments
of those gray Molochs called great cities.

You sometimes reminded me of life's tragedies.
Life seldom let you out of sight.
I think of your generation, crushed by fate,
your illness in Madrid, in Amsterdam
(Hotel Ambassade), even in holy Jerusalem,
the hospital Saint-Louis, where you lay one summer
with heat melting houses' walls and nations' borders,
and your final weeks in Warsaw.
I marvel at your poems' kingly pride.

THE EARLY HOURS

The early hours of morning; you still aren't writing
(rather, you aren't even trying), you just read lazily.
Everything is idle, quiet, full, as if
it were a gift from the muse of sluggishness,

just as earlier, in childhood, on vacation, when a colored
map was slowly scrutinized before a trip, a map
promising so much, deep ponds in the forest
like glittering butterfly eyes, mountain meadows drowning in
      sharp grass;

or the moment before sleep, when no dreams have appeared,
but they whisper their approach from all parts of the world,
their march, their pilgrimage, their vigil at the sickbed
(grown sick of wakefulness), and the quickening among medieval
      figures

compressed in endless stasis over the cathedral;
the early hours of morning, silence
                              —you still aren't writing,
you still understand so much.
                        Joy is close.

SENZA FLASH

Senza flash!: "No flash!"
(order often heard in Italian galleries)

No flame, no sleepless nights, no heat,
no tears, no mighty passions, no convictions,
      and so we live on; senza flash.

Slow and steady, docile, drowsy,
hands stained black from daily papers,
      faces thick with cream; senza flash.

Tourists smiling in their spotless shirts,
Herr Lange and Miss Fee, Monsieur, Madame Rien
      enter the museum; senza flash.

And stand before a Piero della Francesca where
Christ, nearly mad, emerges from the tomb,
      resurrected, free; senza flash.

And something unforeseen may happen then:
hidden in smooth cotton, the heart stirs,
      silence falls, a sudden flash.

CIRCUS

Look, your longing swung from the trapeze.
The clown is you as well and the tame tiger
who begs for mercy calls someone to mind.
Even the tin-pot music
has its charm; it seems
you're starting to make peace
with your times (everyone else has,
why not me?—you say).
So why then does the circus tent
rise above an ancient graveyard?

EUROPE GOES TO SLEEP

To Gosia

Europe goes to sleep; in Lisbon aging
chessplayers still knit their brows.

Gray fog rises over Krakow
and blurs the contours of venerable sails.

The Mediterranean sways lightly
and will be a lullaby soon.

When Europe is sound asleep at last,
America will keep watch

over the poor mute world
mistrustfully, like a younger sister.

A FLAME

God, give us a long winter
and quiet music, and patient mouths,
and a little pride—before
our age ends.
Give us astonishment
and a flame, high, bright.

APARTMENT FOR SCHOLARS

The apartment for visiting scholars holds
a bookshelf with a dozen weary novels in a language
not spoken by your kin, a sleepy Buddha,
a mute TV, a battered skillet bearing traces
of Saturday night's dismal scrambled eggs,

a drab teapot that whistles in every idiom.
You try to settle in and even think.
You read Meister Eckhart about distance (*Abgeschiedenheit*),
the poems of a British Francophile,
an Anglocentric Frenchman's prose;

and only after several days of struggling
to inhabit these hygienic quarters,
hospice to the cream of cultivated humankind,
you realize with something close to awe
that no one lives here; there's no life on earth.

STARY SACZ

A woodpecker in his red cap suddenly brought back
the stationmaster in Stary Sacz.
Over the station rose a little town,
that is, an enormous market and a convent of Poor Clares;
each house had one window holding jars of borscht and pickles.

The innkeeper's daughter was so thin
that she kept bricks in her backpack to outwit the wind
when she crossed the viaduct above the train tracks.
The wind never got her, but other elements weren't idle,
especially Nothingness and her rich suitor, Mr. Time.

BAKERY

A young, ambitious baker in a T-shirt (daubs of flour
on his arms like powder on an actor's face) genially observes
his customers. Smiling slightly. He who knows bread's secret . . .

SUMMER'S FULLNESS

In summer, above a mountain stream scented with willows
where purple butterflies, red admirals, and swallowtails, heavy
    with beauty,
perform their final flight above the glittering water and above
the glittering alder and above the glittering world; where the air
is so drenched in essential oils that you could pour it
into glasses and feel its convex lens beneath your fingers,
in August, when resin burns above the boughs of pines and
    pinecones
crackle as if licked by tongues of everlasting flame,
and a sea authentically blue sways peacefully below
like a victor, a king who's conquered the Persians, and all
his yachts bow gently with every passing wave,
and swimmers submerged in translucent bedding
move with infinite slowness along invisible lines,
along the white threads binding every substance,
and to hear the vast whisper of creatures finally content,
when it seems that even insects must have their own Dionysus,
in August, when Europe's bustle suddenly ceases
and factories stop short, and tourists laugh loudly
on the beaches of the Ligurian Sea, just take two steps
behind the scenes—and there a dense grove's semi-darkness
    may conceal
the shadows of those who lived briefly, in fear, without hope,
    the shadows
of our brothers, our sisters, the shadows of Ravensbrück
    and Kolyma,
poor angels of a black salvation, watching us greedily.

CASTLE

The guards cried out incomprehensibly
in a mountain tribe's guttural dialect.
Venetian windows opened and closed.
Long limousines arrived and left.
Someone seemed to be dying in the palace.
A black banner unfurled,
then drew back like a grass snake's tongue.
Swallows, psalms, grew frantic with worry . . .
But who could it have been,
since the castle had been empty for so long,
given up to bats and irony?
Still everything seemed to indicate
that somebody was dying in the palace.
One couldn't overlook
the signs of life.

DEAD SPARROW

Among all objects
the dead sparrow in its gray topcoat of feathers
is the least unusual.
Even a roadside stone looks like
life's prince when compared
to a dead sparrow.
Flies circle it,
intent as scholars.

MY AUNTS

Always caught up in what they called
the practical side of life
(theory was for Plato),
up to their elbows in furniture, in bedding,
in cupboards and kitchen gardens,
they never neglected the lavender sachets
that turned a linen closet to a meadow.

The practical side of life,
like the Moon's unlighted face,
didn't lack for mysteries;
when Christmastime drew near,
life became pure *praxis*
and resided temporarily in hallways,
took refuge in suitcases and satchels.

And when somebody died—it happened
even in our family, alas—
my aunts, preoccupied
with death's practical side,
forgot at last about the lavender,
whose frantic scent bloomed selflessly
beneath a heavy snow of sheets.

THE CHURCHES OF FRANCE

For Czeslaw Milosz

The churches of France, more welcoming than its inns and its poems,
Standing in vines like great clusters of grapes, or meekly, on hilltops,
Or drowned in valleys, on the floor of a green sea, in a dry
   landscape,
Abandoned buildings, deserted barns
Of gray stone, among gray houses, within gray villages,
But inside pink or white or painted by the sun coming through
   stained glass.
Little Romanesque shrines with stocky frames, like craftsmen shaped
   by their labor,
Pascal's invisible church, sewn into canvas,
And slim cathedrals like herons above the cities, seen clearly from
   the highway, the loveliest is in Chartres,
Where stone stifles desire.
The mills of the Cistercians, turning water in Sunday streams, and
   their ponds,
Synagogues, elder sisters, betrayed and plundered so often, discreet,
The ruined abbey in Normandy, where among the raspberry
   bushes a black adder basks in the heat,
A small tree, growing on the roof of a village church, a young ash
   that will become a monk,
The basilica in Vézelay, belonging to Magdalene, pink as a wild
   strawberry's mouth.
Claudel's church, thickset, almost neckless, inspired, sometimes
   full of spite
And the church in Tournus, whose arches must make the Arabs
   proud too,
The moss-covered walls of modest chapels that have forgotten
   their names
And the fortified basilica in Albi, a masterwork of military art,
   sheathed in a dragon's skin,

And in the square the peddlers of nuts, holy pictures, and aniseed
    cakes.
But at night the peddlers vanish and only walls and windows,
    blind as kittens, remain,
And the vast night and much silence and sometimes a dying
    comet's roar.
Romanesque columns in cloisters, as if carved by brilliant children.
Meadows, where lovers meet.
The stone Jeremiah in Moissac, with a kind face.
The church of Maurice, who learned my language and lives in
    Warsaw among the poorest.
The churches of France, dark vessels, where the shy flame of a
    mighty light wanders.

WHERE THE BREATH IS

She stands alone onstage
and has no instrument.

She lays her palms upon her breast,
where the breath is born
and where it dies.

The palms do not sing,
nor does the breast.

What sings is what stays silent.

SPEAK SOFTLY . . .

Speak softly: you're older than the one
you were so long; you're older
than yourself—and yet you still don't know
what absence, poetry, and gold are.

Rusty water swept the street; a brief storm
shook this supine, sleepy city.
Each storm is a valediction, scores of photographers
seem to swirl above us, catching in a flash
our moments of panic and fear.

You know what mourning is, despair so fierce
it chokes the heart's rhythm and the future.
You've cried among strangers, in a modern store,
where deft coins make the rounds.

You've seen Venice and Siena and, in paintings, on the streets,
doleful young Madonnas, who wish they were
ordinary girls dancing at carnivals.

You've also seen small towns, not beautiful at all,
old people, worn by pain and time.
Eyes shone in medieval icons,
the eyes of swarthy saints, wild animals' bright eyes.

You picked dry pebbles from the beach at la Galère,
and suddenly you felt as fond of them
—of them and the slender pine,
and everyone else there, and the sea,
which is powerful indeed, but very lonely—

as if we all were orphans
from the same home, parted for good
and granted only momentary visits
in the chilly prisons of the present.

Speak softly: you're no longer young,
revelation must make peace with weeks of Lent,
you must choose, surrender, stall for time,

hold long talks with envoys from dry countries
and cracked lips, you must wait,
write letters, read books of five hundred pages.
Speak softly. Don't give up on poetry.

LINE FOUR

I only write about the dead,
one beggar said.
Summer will be starting soon.
On the Porte de Clignancourt–
Porte d'Orléans line you always catch the odor
of burnt paper; an inquisitive rat
at the Saint-Michel stop seems to ask:
what century is this, dear sirs and madams?
I waded slowly through this day.
Once again I missed what's most important.

GEORGES SEURAT: *FACTORY*

(a drawing in the de Menil Collection, Houston)

For Jacek Waltos

In the mountains, on the map's edge, where the grass is brash and
    sharp as deserters' bayonets, a forgotten factory rises.
We don't know if it's dawn or dusk. We only know one thing:
    here, in this glum building, light is being born.
Silent slaves with the narrow, transparent faces of Byzantine
    monks turn an enormous dynamo and ignite the golden
    sparks of dawn in the globe's farthest reaches. Some cry,
    others smoke stylish cigarettes as light as a sparrow's breath.
    They don't answer questions: their tongues have been cut out.
Right beneath the wall, where the black weeds grow, darkness has
    hidden. It's absolutely still. The world's hair grows.

THE POLISH BIOGRAPHICAL DICTIONARY
IN A LIBRARY IN HOUSTON

Prince Roman Sanguszko treks across Siberia
(Joseph Conrad will write a story about him).
Near the end of his long life he founds a library;
he dies universally admired.

Maria Kalergis (see: Muchanow, Maria)
—alleged ties with the Tsar's secret police;
"half her heart is Polish," the other half—
unknown. Friends with Liszt and Wagner,

Chopin's pupil. Patron of the Warsaw theater,
renegade and patriot by turns.
Penniless Norwid fell in love with her (see: Norwid).
And loved her with all his heart.

Julian Klaczko: "Short, rather heavy-set
. . . high-strung, excitable. No lack
of self-esteem" (Stanislaw Tarnowski).
Perhaps the natural son of the ill-famed Pelikan.

A sparkling stylist, the glory of *La Revue des Deux Mondes*.
Worked with the Czartoryskis, then employed
by the Austrian ministry (there was no Polish one).
He expires in Krakow, paralyzed, already dead.

So many more: Antoni Czapski (*1792),
studied painting in England and France, a mason
in the lodge of Chaste Sarmatians: virtue personified.
Joachim Namysl, educator—we've reached the twentieth century.

Still more shadows, A to S;
this dictionary cannot be completed.

This is your country, your laconism.
Your indifference and your emotion.

So much life for just one homeland.
So much death for just one dictionary.

JUST CHILDREN

For Ewunia

It was just children playing in the sand
(accompanied by the narcotic scent
of blooming lindens, don't forget),
just children, but after all
the devil, and the minor gods,
and even forgotten politicians,
who'd broken all their promises,
were also there and watched them
with unending rapture.
Who wouldn't want to be a child
—for the last time!

A MORNING IN VICENZA

In memoriam Joseph Brodsky, Krzysztof Kieslowski

The sun was so fragile, so young,
that we were a little scared; a careless move
might scratch it, just a shout—if anyone
had tried—might do it harm; only the rushing swifts,
with wings hard as cast-iron,
were free to sing out loud, because they'd spent their brief,
uneasy childhoods in clay nests
alongside siblings, small, mad planets,
black as forest berries.

In a small café the sleepy waiter—the night's last shadows
met beneath his eyes—searched for change
in his vast pocket, and the coffee smelled of solemn
printer's ink, of sweetness, Arabia. The sky's blue
promised a long afternoon, an endless day.
I saw you as if for the first time.
And even the Palladio columns seemed
newborn, they rose from waves of dawn
like Venus, your elder companion.

To start from scratch, to count the losses, count the dead,
to start a new day without the two of you, first you
whom we buried twice and lamented twice,
you lived two times as strongly as the rest, on two continents,
in two languages, in the world and in imagination—then you,
with your chiseled face, the gaze that amplified
objects and hearts (always too small).
You both are gone, and so from now we'll lead a double life,
at once in shadow and in light, in bright sunshine
and the cool of stony halls, in mourning and in joy.

EUROPE IN WINTER

For Anders Bodegård

When the dirty snow buries your treasures,
when your mammoth cathedrals, now
holding five old ladies, are lost in fog
and planes flying just above the trees
start grumbling like tugboats
in the gruff bass of a Russian emigrant,
when the holiday hordes, possessed
by one urge only, the urge for yellow gold,
throng the broad, damp boulevards,
and your museums are shut down by strikes,

and the low sky like the frayed drape
of a sad painter covers the uncommon places
where your saints lived, and your
inspired artists, your madmen and your monks—
I'll see your river flowing upstream, northwards,
and your wingless poplars; the chestnut vendors
will call out, while the peddlers of white papers
will silently proffer their flat epics—
I'll try to enter your streets, I'll try to enter
the low courtyards of your aging houses,

to enter the underworld of your Métro, where
Persephone died of longing, and the
poor districts, where virtue and vice
stroll gravely, like Laurel and Hardy,
I'll try to track the addresses of torment and ecstasy,
the final shreds of your vocation,
I'll try to retrieve the noble song
that takes flight like swift balloons
from children's hands, I'll try to find your love,
a fragment of your faith.

DEATH OF A PIANIST

While others waged war
or sued for peace, or lay
in narrow beds in hospitals
or camps, for days on end

he practiced Beethoven's sonatas,
and slim fingers, like a miser's,
touched great treasures
that weren't his.

DECEMBER

December, herald of destruction,
takes you on a long walk
through the black torsos of trees
and leaves scorched by the autumn's fire,

as if saying: see what's left
of your secrets, your treasures,
the febrile trill of little birds,
the promises of summer months.

Your dreams have been dissected,
the blackbirds' song now has a rationale,
plants' corpses adorn the herbariums.
Only the laboratory's hard nut remains.

Don't listen: they may take everything,
but they can't have your ignorance,
they'll leave your mysteries, won't uncover
your third homeland.

Don't listen, the holidays approach,
and frozen January, snow's white paper.
What you await is just now being born.
The one you're seeking will begin to sing.

VAPORETTO

In the windbreaker's pocket you find
a light blue ticket for the vaporetto
(il biglietto, non cedibile).

A light blue ticket, slightly larger
than a stamp from the republic of Togo,
promises a change, a journey.

Sealing wax melts on a memory,
the almond of alpine snow thaws.
The expedition may proceed.

You're in Texas, on flat land,
surrounded by evergreen oaks
that remember nothing.

You'll sail through cramped canals
upstream, in a strong wind;
you'll meet with icebergs, grayness.

The ticket says: *corsa semplice*,
but not a word about the desert,
the monotony of heavy seas,

about longing, or the spiteful customs man
who's waiting, and not for you alone,
about islands of indifference and ash.

You'll swim a long time. And maybe reach
the place where the sea urchin Venice rests:
water, lace, and gold.

You may reach the place where Venice's
red towers rise, faithful towers,
the needles of a compass lost at sea.

The train stopped in a field; the sudden silence
startled even sleep's most ardent partisans.
The distant lights of shops or factories
glittered in the haze like the yellow eyes of wolves.
Businessmen on trips stooped over their computers,
totting up the day's losses and gains.
The stewardess poured coffee steeped in bitterness.
Ewig, ewig, last word, *Song of the Earth*,
it repeats so often; remember how we listened
to this music, to the promise that
we so longed to believe.

We don't know if we're still in Holland,
this may be Belgium now. No matter.
An early winter evening, and the earth hid
beneath thick streaks of dusk; you could
sense the presence of a canal's black water,
unmoving, stripped of mountain currents' joy
and the great amazement of our oceans.
Wolves' yellow eyes were quivering with a nervous
neon light, but no one feared an Indian attack.
The train stopped at that moment when our reason starts
to stir, but the soul, its noble yearning, is asleep.

We were listening a different time to Schubert,
that posthumous quintet where despair declares itself
insistently, intently, almost insatiably,
renewing its assault on the indifference
of the genteel concert hall, ladies in their furs
and the reviewers, minor envoys of the major papers.

And once out walking, midnight, summer in the country,
a strange sound stopped us short: snorting and neighing
of unseen horses in a pasture. As though
the night laughed happily to itself.
What is poetry if we see so little?

What is salvation if there is no threat?
Posthumous quintet! Only music keeps on growing
after death, music and the hair of trees.
As if rivers gave ecstatic milk and honey,
as if dancers danced in frenzy once again . . .
And yet we're not alone. One day some guitar
worn by time will start singing for itself alone.
And the train moves at last, the earth rocks
underneath its stately weight and slowly
Paris draws close, with its golden aura,
its gray doubt.

TWENTY-FIVE YEARS

To my sister, Ewa

Your dream pulsed in the depths of time,
a calm, light breath: so travelers sleep
when overtaken by a brief storm at a station
in Tuscany, in a town with dust and wasps.

You'd be twenty-five now,
listening to those songs that I can't stand,
maybe nursing a newly broken heart,
and I'd be busy making fun of you.

Your calm dream pulses in time's depths;
children forgotten by their nurse sleep on like this,
and never waken, and don't leave
the underwater rooms where dolphins weep.

HOW CLOWNS GO

An old clown hands out flyers at the station
for a traveling circus. No doubt
this is how clowns go—replacing vending machines (or children).
I watch him carefully: I want to know how clowns go.

The captivating balance between sadness
and mad, infectious laughter slowly slips;
each year the furrow in the cheeks grows deeper.
What's left is the desperately oversized nose

and an old man's clumsiness—not a parody
of healthy, silly humans, but a broadside
on the body's flaws, the builder's
errors. What's left is the large gleaming forehead, a lamp

made of white cheese (not painted now), thin lips
and eyes from which a stranger coldly
gazes, perhaps the face's next tenant—
if the lease on this grief can be renewed.

This is how clowns go—when the world's great indifference
invades us, enters us bitterly, like lead between our teeth.

HOW HIGH THE MOON

Of course there were
the family trips in summer,
picnics by a black canal

(named earlier for Adolf Hitler)
where crabs still lived;
on its banks the pines were gaunt and stunted.

Sometimes—rarely—barges holding coal,
like charcoal for a Sunday painter,
sailed due west.

The heat wave changed clothes like an opera star:
sky-blue, rosy, scarlet,
finally white, transparent.

My uncle supervised
our outings: he loved life
(but it wasn't mutual).

If anyone had told me then
that this was childhood,
I would have said no;

it was just hours and days,
endless hours,
the sweet days of June

on the banks of a canal
that never rushed,
drenched in damp dreams,

and the meek young moon
setting out alone
to vanquish night.

TARBES

Palms grow in the garden where
they buried winter. The Pyrenees' shadow
sways on the horizon.
Anything can happen.
Dusty houses, closed windows.
Thrushes hidden in the paulownia's branches
sing thrillingly each evening,
while night enters the streets from the east
like the Foreign Legion.

LITTLE WALTZ

The days are so vivid, so bright
that even the slim, sparse palms
are covered in the white dust of neglect.
Serpents in the vineyards slither softly,
but the evening sea grows dark and,
suspended overhead like punctuation
in the highest script, the seagulls barely stir.
A drop of wine's inscribed upon your lips.
The limestone hills slowly melt
on the horizon and a star appears.
At night on the square an orchestra of sailors
dressed in spotless white
plays a little waltz by Shostakovich; small children
cry as if they'd guessed
what the merry music's really saying.
We've been locked in the world's box,
love sets us free, time kills us.

SUNRISE OVER CASSIS

In the semi-darkness white buildings loom, not fully
formulated, and beside them, the gray vineyards, the quiet before
    dawn;
Judas counts his silver coins, but olive trees contorted
in wild prayer enter the earth ever more deeply.
Where is the sun! But it's still cold
and a humble landscape spreads around us;
the stars have gone and priests sleep tight, birds aren't allowed
to sing in August and only now and then one
stammers like a lazy boy in high school Latin.
It's four a.m. and despair lives in so many houses.
This is the time when sad philosophers with narrow faces
compose their jaded aphorisms and worn conductors,
who'd brought Bruckner and Mahler back to life that evening,
drift off to sleep unwilling, unapplauded, and whores go home
to their shabby apartments.
                      We ask that the vineyards,
gray as if coated with volcanic ash, be given life,
and that the great, distant cities awaken from their apathy,
and I ask not to confuse freedom with chaos
and to regain the faith that unites
things seen and unseen, but doesn't lull the heart.
Beneath us the sea turns blue and the horizon's line
grows ever finer, like a slender fillet
that embraces, lovingly and firmly, our turning planet,
and we see fishing boats rock trustfully like gulls
upon the deep, blue waters and a moment later
the sun's crimson disc emerges from a half circle of hills
and returns the gift of light.

Gombrowicz died; Americans walked on the Moon,
hopping cautiously, as though it might break.
Erbarme dich, mein Gott, one black woman sang
in a certain church.
Summer scorched us, the lake water was warm and sweet.
The cold war dragged on, the Russians occupied Prague.
We met for the first time that year.
Only the grass, worn and yellow, was immortal.
Gombrowicz died. Americans walked on the Moon.
Have mercy, time. Have mercy, destruction.

THE WORLD'S PROSE

Die Prosa der Welt
—Hegel, of course

Imagine a day begun in Le Bon Café;
colored newspapers on tables and Aznavour's songs come
drifting from the speakers. A brief moment of attention:
the coquettish French "r" whirls like a child's plaything
within the mighty city, the empire's hub,
and seems about to thaw the winter's queen.
Nervous bureaucrats in narrow suits
gulp scalding coffee, the liquid of oblivion.
Four solitary airplanes circle overhead.

I stand before the picture Rilke talks of:
a family of acrobats has turned up in a desert.
No one's watching, and their many tricks
and songs, concealed in tambourines and supple muscles,
their leaps and jokes all go for nothing here.
They gaze uncertainly, they look around;
the young woman on the far right would like
to leave the painting (she stands apart).
They look around, but what is there to see?

Snow lies around us, covering the architecture of power.
Snow wraps the monumental shapes with slipcases
and even the narrow heads of obelisks have turned white.
Provincial trees breathe quietly beneath the snow,
and fresh leaf buds sleep tight, waiting for a sign.
You pay with life for every moment of snow, for
what is white and what is black, for happiness, for seeing.
The prose of life spreads out around us,
while poetry crouches in the heart's chambers.

A KING

In memory of Jozef Czapski

He was very old. But his spirit held.
Of one acquaintance (old as he) he said:
"That famed Petersburg beauty; observe
her face." He still painted. Lived. Wrote. Thought.

He knew Akhmatova. Spoke with de Gaulle,
André Malraux also took note.
Gide (too Parisian) disappointed him.
A penniless count, he helped the poor.

So tall (and good), as if proud
nature wished to put him on display.
Mary McCarthy once glimpsed him in a crowd
at a museum and jotted down: a righteous man.

Beauty thrilled him. He spoke
more often though of ugliness and pain—
things it seems he scarcely knew
(but how can we be sure?)

What's the moment when divinity appears?
How can we tell, since we always keep it
in the past tense or the future (hopefully!)
We describe it from a distant country,

where we've been carried by a wild express train
with no stops at that small still station
we call Beauty, a resting place
too modest for its taste.

But we can talk of ugliness
at length, and pain will still fill
many tomes; our quick sightseeing trip
becomes a humble tortoise city tram.

His death was long and patient; perhaps those
who rule the earth and play at chess demurred:
should such a splendid upright shape, a king,
be made a horizontal form, a line of print?

SMOKE

Too many elegies. Too much memory.
The scent of hay and a white heron
flies uncertainly across a field.
We know how to bury the dead.
We don't want to kill.
But potent moments of light
elude our spells.
My room is heaped with dreams
piled high like rugs
inside a stuffy Oriental shop
and there is no room for new poems now.
The roe deer won't take flight,
she tries to prophesy.
No one pays homage to the gods.
An angry prayer is stronger.
Linden flowers, an open wound.
Smoke rises over low-lying towns
and peace enters our homes;
our homes fill with wholeness.

LINDENS

So much sweetness—
the city's been anesthetized;
a skinny boy, who barely
takes up space on earth,
and a dog,
and I, a soldier in an unseen war,
and a river I love.
The lindens bloom.

SEPARATION

I read almost with envy my contemporaries' verse:
divorces, partings, wrenching separations;
anguish, new beginnings, minor deaths;
letters read and burned, burning, reading, fire, culture,
anger and despair—the very stuff of potent poems;
stern verdicts, mocking laughter of the lofty moralists,
then finally the triumph of the all-enduring self.

And for us? No elegies, no sonnets about parting,
a poem's screen won't rise between us,
apt metaphors can't sever us,
the only separation that we don't escape is sleep,
sleep's deep cave, where we descend alone
—and I must keep in mind that the hand
I'm clasping then is made of dreams.

In a bookstore I accidentally ended up at the section on Tao, or
more precisely, by the *Treatise on Emptiness*.
I rejoiced, since that day I was perfectly empty.
What an unexpected meeting—the patient finds the doctor,
the doctor doesn't speak.

SÉNANQUE

The weary tourists seek illumination
and explore the refectory's dark nooks;
someone's sleeping in the sun, his open lips

are entered by Provence's splendid
air, oxygen and herbs, herbs and oxygen,
and the earth's dry breath.

Now and then a stern figure flits by—
in a habit, he has no time,
he's got time only for eternity.

These thick walls, guarding music,
destroyed so many times, given up to nature,
revolution, reason, grow anew.

Fields of lavender surround the cloister—
armies of bees and the young spring buzz above them,
and, slowly, golden heedfulness is born.

BARBARIANS

We were the barbarians.
You trembled before us in your palaces.
You awaited us with pounding hearts.
You commented on our languages:
they apparently consist of consonants alone,
of rustles, whispers, and dry leaves.
We were those who lived in the dark forests.
We were what Ovid feared in Tomi,
we were the worshippers of gods with names
you could not pronounce.
But we too knew loneliness
and fear, and began longing for poetry.

FOR YOU

It's not the only poem—are you asleep now
in a cloud of woolen dreams—I've written for you.
For you, triumphant, smiling, lovely,
but also for you, conquered and subdued,

(although I've never understood
who could defeat you!),
for you, mistrustful and uneasy,
I've written poem after poem,

as if hoping one day—like the tortoise
—to reach, by way of faulty words
and images, the place where you have been so long,
where life's lightning carried you.

ANCIENT HISTORY

It was one of those evenings when the clouds,
powerful as transatlantic steamers,
do friendly battle with the sun, and the light,
the keen, relentless light of June,
endures unending changes and filtrations.
And since the city was vast, thousands of people
returned to the suburbs
by train or car
after a day of useless labor
like toy soldiers in cardboard boxes
packed with fresh hay.
But the ancient world lay hidden underfoot,
Greeks with the broken noses of boxers,
sullen, silent, hungry.
High above the chimneys and antennas that sprouted
from shimmering tin roofs, a rainstorm circled
but couldn't bring itself to strike.
Beyond the rainstorm the beaming deity
of this evening, this world, lay sprawled.
Beyond the deity was nothing,
just an earnest blackbird singing its ecstatic song.
I stood stock-still on the street, pinned
by desire, partly painful, partly sweet,
and prayed, ineptly,
for myself and others,
for my mother, who had died,
and for my death,
an untamed animal.

FOR GABRIELA MÜNTER

Winter was mild that year,
the houses' scarlet spots weren't frozen,
they hadn't faded yet and apples are so sensitive.
The ruddy beech remembers summer's sweetness
and wolves don't dare approach the altars
of our dark apartments.
Beyond the wall you hear somebody breathing.
We know only this: life is warm.
But the masts of sailing ships and thin antennas
already tremble,
wine pours from jugs
and this quiet valley, hidden from
the hunters' sight, may drown;
will surely drown, Gabriela.

SQUARE D'ORLÉANS

A place where pain and beauty
mingled once—two substances
that have long been acquainted.
A bank now occupies this space;
dapper gentlemen enter and exit,
each one slim as a new banknote.

Chopin lived here once. His fingers
struck the keyboard, matter, in a rage.
Impassioned poetry once lived here.
Peace and quiet now prevail, while nearby
insurance agents flourish, and the doctor
receives his patients at appointed hours.

Dusk falls; apartment houses stand
like worried herons on the century's rubble
(the distant whistle of the city sounds).
In the center of the square a little fountain
shyly raises up two braids of water,
reminding us of what life really is.

We sit on the steps as nothing happens.
It's also impossible to say
that we feel anything like sorrow.
Anxiety and frenzy (two
younger nations) have given way
to classical restraint.

The September evening slowly darkens,
a gentle wind traverses Paris
like an elderly Kabuki actor
playing the ingenue's part.
If anything upsets us—but nothing
does—it's only emptiness.

TRY TO PRAISE THE MUTILATED WORLD

Try to praise the mutilated world.
Remember June's long days,
and wild strawberries, drops of rosé wine.
The nettles that methodically overgrow
the abandoned homesteads of exiles.
You must praise the mutilated world.
You watched the stylish yachts and ships;
one of them had a long trip ahead of it,
while salty oblivion awaited others.
You've seen the refugees going nowhere,
you've heard the executioners sing joyfully.
You should praise the mutilated world.
Remember the moments when we were together
in a white room and the curtain fluttered.
Return in thought to the concert where music flared.
You gathered acorns in the park in autumn
and leaves eddied over the earth's scars.
Praise the mutilated world
and the gray feather a thrush lost,
and the gentle light that strays and vanishes
and returns.

EARLY POEMS

(1970–1975)

TRANSLATED BY CLARE CAVANAGH

THE NAME EDMUND

Edmund Husserl, modern philosopher,
Plato's friend, and Edmund Monsiel,
ailing mill worker,
two Jews from Western and
Central Europe, are dead now and anyone
may give his son that name
without a thought
to the little violet face
that expands all the drawings
of Monsiel and is also the image,
slightly altered, of Husserl.

THE EPICURE FROM MY STAIRCASE

The epicure from my staircase
who's taken evening classes
in Marxism-Leninism
who's completed an accelerated course in love
lets his mother-in-law out
twice daily a sick old lady
who spits old black blood
and calls him you son-of-a-bitch
Then he points his radio at her
which happens to be broadcasting
a program on modern youth full blast
and he thinks I'm still young
my life spreads before me
like a bay in summer's bright sun

TONGUE

Shut in a white cage
At the slightest breath of air
it tries to flee
It's caught after a few letters
Its flights in Polish
receive the most lenient treatment
Even so the mouth's cruelty
defies description
The tongue is the last animal
in the face's reservation.

TRUTH

Arise open the doors untie the cords
free yourself from the nerves' net
you're Jonah who consumes the whale
Refuse to shake hands with that man
stand straight drain the tampon of the tongue
abandon this cocoon tear these membranes
inhale the deepest layers of the air
and slowly remembering the laws of syntax
tell the truth that's what you serve in your left hand
you hold love in your right hatred

Letters I never answered
answer each other
Books I never read
open their seven wounds

If you live in the world's center
you must account for everything
The living and the dead are watching you

I can't tell the living from the dead now
so many die
I just don't know if Pablo Picasso provincial painter
is alive if his countless victims are still living
If Thomas Mann who visited his novels' heroes
in the hospital is still living
The Jewish saint from Drohobycz who is he today
where are the fiancées of the great martyrs
who loved them so much they
couldn't marry them
But you
live
in the world's center
the dead are on the right hand
there are no living yet

You remember all those places
great rooms with wedding photos of the masters
a painted Jesus who makes his first
communion in a suit of thorns
you remember the Africas of beds the cold
rectangles of hotel floors

all the forbidden places
sickly women who stuck out
the white fingers of their tongues to take the last
sacrament of love and asked which road
as if they didn't know they were at home
breathing behind walls hurried departures
you remember those who preserved their
faces with scars of lips that never healed
you remember fighters from under lakes and rivers
knights who spit their noble blood
in public and also those
who hid their wounds beneath a gauze of death
but it was all so obvious
that waiters died laughing

Those born after the first war
wouldn't shake my hand at party
meetings they voted with spread palms
webbed between the fingers
Skarga returned his party card and left the hall
the fox and lamb pursued him with a spear
in their side that suddenly blossomed and the chase stopped
Those born on the war's last day
have ordinary human hands
Those born on the war's last day
still don't know the art of double love
You remember the springtime of the poets
whose beards were shaved at the gates
it wasn't thought proper for young poets to look so
old it was thought that beards deform young faces
Some stopped writing others sailed through
Europe's overflowing heart sent letters home
walls of barracks housing projects
were trimmed with mistletoe winter drew close
a new world was beginning

I admit I didn't see the flames fewer insects all the time
I admit repellent blind men can't be seen
a film of sand conceals the blood of crashes
everybody looks the same
and each night the same drunken stammering unites
the nation's workers
I admit knives sleep in sheaths
you live in Krakow you're a poet
you live in Szczecin beneath a face's ax
you're a docker who lives in the world's center
the dead are on the right hand
there are no living yet

Don't be lulled by soccer leagues
you played yourself once now an old animal
you watch the ball's flight with unmoving eyes
and shake the dandruff from your collar don't
be lulled by the soft taste of summer nights
when women bear their steaming bodies out of doors
don't be lulled by the cool water of spas
there's a wilderness nearby and every step you take
leaves a trace that cannot be erased
Fins grow back on trees don't
be lulled by tame birds
A missile will emerge from every bird when it begins
again and feeding the pigeons doesn't help
they can't be bought don't be lulled
by weary aging leaders dust on portraits
A young leader will emerge from every old one
a hangman sewn into his body's uniform don't be lulled
by his barely literate diploma
they can err at any moment lawns become
volcanoes a tank will emerge from every car
don't be lulled by Freud's lingering
execution in London and long speeches' tedium

Don't doze off listening to the evening news
your neighbor never sleeps it isn't love
that makes him weak don't be lulled
by his clumsy speech what he explains
so awkwardly each day was laid out long ago
I'm not thinking about war you even like it the best
boys perish while you go upstairs
to write your memoirs I'm not thinking about war
don't let that lull you there are so many
hidden wars anything can happen
each house conceals a second
hidden house your every move
might be a different one everything you say
could be said differently you could have
different friends you might never have met just
that one woman you could have met a different one
don't be lulled by the smile pinned
to her face like a wing your every thought
could be somebody else's you might not
have met her you could think the opposite
the same as me and you'd like
your ideas even more
don't be lulled by the wrinkle on your forehead
everything's on loan
don't be lulled by your new apartment
and your picture in the paper no resemblance
to yourself doubly on loan
you stand at strict attention so what
you're naked and in every dream the old man
you really are comes home
Don't let poems lull you
just don't read them you haven't got time
time's got you grips you in its fist
its claws if it's a bird
chokes you slowly you think it's only asthma

don't be lulled by the doctors' Internationale
Anything can happen
what's normal ends quickest
it's so easy to grasp what isn't normal
so easy to make peace with it
don't be lulled by that ease

I admit that sunny skies prevail
hotels like gardens teem with ruddy
cheeks of cheery men on formal
delegations they seek official seals
submit to complex operations under the care
of women grown thin with happiness
but next time one of them may not return
the investigations will begin
Stanley will return to Africa
Nobile will fly back to the pole
man-made satellites won't blink an eye
Gagarin will part with his mother
Socrates will stand before the court
Columbus will be torn from his bed in the dead of night
so many perished
that I can't remember who's still living
and who has just now died.

HOW DOES THE MAN LOOK WHO'S RIGHT

How does the man look who's right
what kind of tie does he wear
does he speak in complete sentences
does he dress in well-worn clothes
did he walk out of a sea of blood or
a sea of oblivion do his clothes still
bear traces of sharp-tasting salt
what era is this man from
is his skin sallow
does he cry in his sleep what does he dream of
always this same room
with the wall's extracted heart does he talk
to himself does he live in an old man's
rented body how much unrest
does this cubicle cost him is he an exile
from what city is it curiosity
that drives him is it worth it
who answers for this what's that stain
on his coat who stands behind him
could you tell him that everything is
relative depending on how you look at it
no one knows how it really is
see if you can recognize him
as he crosses the street
hunched beneath the weight of brains

TWENTY-YEAR-OLD SOLDIERS

I couldn't paint, my voice cracked,
I didn't pass the high school finals,
I couldn't be an artist. They assigned me
to the infantry, the second unit of the fatherland's
sons, we cleaned our weapons and listened
to peacetime speeches, the war dragged on,
the closed eyes of houses watched revolts
of animals and endless processions
of sacrificial elders, my mother brought me
bread hiding newspapers from the time of the great hunger
for truth, I gave the bread to friends, and used the paper
to build warships, great battles and unintended
victories awaited us,
rumbling wagons and the cries of drunk commanders
woke us at night, we were certain,
twenty-year-old soldiers, that
the true army drew nearer, craving blood.

PHILOSOPHERS

Stop deceiving us philosophers
work is not a joy man is not the highest goal
work is deadly sweat Lord when I get home
I'd like to sleep but sleep's just a driving belt
transporting me to the next day and the sun's a fake
coin morning rips my eyelids sealed as before
birth my hands are two *Gastarbeiter* and even
my tears don't belong to me they participate in public life
like speakers with chapped lips and a heart that's
grown into the brain
Work is not a joy but incurable pain
like a disease of the open conscience like new housing projects
through which the citizen wind passes
in his high leather boots

IMMORTALITY

These poor nineteenth-century poets
dreamers with flushed cheeks
our great brothers ablaze with
inspiration allowed their portraits to be made
in Paris stars today of school anthologies
and authors of quotes that justify
every injustice

FROM

TREMOR

(1985)

TRANSLATED BY RENATA GORCZYNSKI

TO GO TO LVOV

To go to Lvov. Which station
for Lvov, if not in a dream, at dawn, when dew
gleams on a suitcase, when express
trains and bullet trains are being born. To leave
in haste for Lvov, night or day, in September
or in March. But only if Lvov exists,
if it is to be found within the frontiers and not just
in my new passport, if lances of trees
—of poplar and ash—still breathe aloud
like Indians, and if streams mumble
their dark Esperanto, and grass snakes like soft signs
in the Russian language disappear
into thickets. To pack and set off, to leave
without a trace, at noon, to vanish
like fainting maidens. And burdocks, green
armies of burdocks, and below, under the canvas
of a Venetian café, the snails converse
about eternity. But the cathedral rises,
you remember, so straight, as straight
as Sunday and white napkins and a bucket
full of raspberries standing on the floor, and
my desire which wasn't born yet,
only gardens and weeds and the amber
of Queen Anne cherries, and indecent Fredro.
There was always too much of Lvov, no one could
comprehend its boroughs, hear
the murmur of each stone scorched
by the sun, at night the Orthodox church's silence was unlike
that of the cathedral, the Jesuits
baptized plants, leaf by leaf, but they grew,
grew so mindlessly, and joy hovered

everywhere, in hallways and in coffee mills
revolving by themselves, in blue
teapots, in starch, which was the first
formalist, in drops of rain and in the thorns
of roses. Frozen forsythia yellowed by the window.
The bells pealed and the air vibrated, the cornets
of nuns sailed like schooners near
the theater, there was so much of the world that
it had to do encores over and over,
the audience was in frenzy and didn't want
to leave the house. My aunts couldn't have known
yet that I'd resurrect them,
and lived so trustfully, so singly;
servants, clean and ironed, ran for
fresh cream, inside the houses
a bit of anger and great expectation, Brzozowski
came as a visiting lecturer, one of my
uncles kept writing a poem entitled *Why*,
dedicated to the Almighty, and there was too much
of Lvov, it brimmed the container,
it burst glasses, overflowed
each pond, lake, smoked through every
chimney, turned into fire, storm,
laughed with lightning, grew meek,
returned home, read the New Testament,
slept on a sofa beside the Carpathian rug,
there was too much of Lvov, and now
there isn't any, it grew relentlessly
and the scissors cut it, chilly gardeners
as always in May, without mercy,
without love, ah, wait till warm June
comes with soft ferns, boundless
fields of summer, i.e., the reality.
But scissors cut it, along the line and through
the fiber, tailors, gardeners, censors

cut the body and the wreaths, pruning shears worked
diligently, as in a child's cutout
along the dotted line of a roe deer or a swan.
Scissors, penknives, and razor blades scratched,
cut, and shortened the voluptuous dresses
of prelates, of squares and houses, and trees
fell soundlessly, as in a jungle,
and the cathedral trembled, people bade goodbye
without handkerchiefs, no tears, such a dry
mouth, I won't see you anymore, so much death
awaits you, why must every city
become Jerusalem and every man a Jew,
and now in a hurry just
pack, always, each day,
and go breathless, go to Lvov, after all
it exists, quiet and pure as
a peach. It is everywhere.

A WANDERER

I enter the waiting room in a station.
Not a breath of air.
                       I have a book in my pocket,
someone's poems, traces of inspiration.
At the entrance, on benches, two tramps and a drunkard
(or two drunkards and a tramp).
At the other end, an elderly couple, very elegant, sit
staring somewhere above them, toward Italy and the sky.
We have always been divided. Mankind, nations,
waiting rooms.
                 I stop for a moment,
uncertain which suffering I should
join.
       Finally, I take a seat in between
and start reading. I am alone but not lonely.
A wanderer who doesn't wander.
                       The revelation
flickers and dies. Mountains of breath, close
valleys. The dividing goes on.

ODE TO SOFTNESS

Mornings are blind as newborn cats.
Fingernails grow so trustfully, for a while
they don't know what they're going to touch. Dreams
are soft, and tenderness looms over us
like fog, like the cathedral bell of Krakow
before it cooled.

LATE BEETHOVEN

I haven't yet known a man who loved virtue as strongly as one loves beauty.

—Confucius

Nobody knows who she was, the Immortal
Beloved. Apart from that, everything is
clear. Feathery notes rest
peacefully on the threads of the staff
like martins just come
from the Atlantic. What would I have to be
in order to speak about him, he who's still
growing. Now we are walking alone
without ghosts or banners. Long live
chaos, say our solitary mouths.
We know that he dressed carelessly,
that he was given to fits of avarice, that he wasn't
always fair to his friends.
Friends are a hundred years
late with their impeccable smiles. Who
was the Immortal Beloved? Certainly,
he loved virtue more than beauty.
But a nameless god of beauty dwelled
in him and compelled his obedience.
He improvised for hours. A few minutes
of each improvisation were noted down.
These minutes belong neither to the nineteenth
nor to the twentieth century; as if hydrochloric
acid burned a window in velvet, thus
opening a passage to even
smoother velvet, thin as
a spiderweb. Now they name
ships and perfumes after him. They don't know who
the Immortal Beloved was, otherwise
new cities and pâtés would bear her
name. But it's useless. Only velvet

growing under velvet, like a leaf hidden
safely in another leaf. Light in darkness.
Unending adagios. That's how tired freedom
breathes. Biographers argue only
over details. Why he tormented
his nephew Karl so much. Why
he walked so fast. Why he didn't go
to London. Apart from that, everything is clear.
We don't know what music is. Who speaks
in it. To whom it is addressed. Why it is
so obstinately silent. Why it circles and returns
instead of giving a straight answer
as the Gospel demands. Prophecies
were not fulfilled. The Chinese didn't reach
the Rhine. Once more, it turned out that
the real world doesn't exist, to the immense
relief of antiquaries. The secret was hidden
somewhere else, not in soldiers'
knapsacks, but in a few notebooks.
Grillparzer, he, Chopin. Generals are
cast in lead and in tinsel to
give hell's flame a moment of respite
after kilowatts of straw. Unending adagios,
but first and foremost joy, wild
joy of shape, the laughing sister of death.

SCHOPENHAUER'S CRYING

Yes, it is the same Schopenhauer (1788–
1860), the author of *The World as Will
and Representation*, discoverer of nature's
guile and the Music of the Spheres. Later,
someone will call him the teacher. Nothing has happened
because nothing happens. It's just a certain
child, a brat who slightly resembles
a woman he knew in his youth—
youth doesn't exist—a child who smiled at him
to no avail, being, probably,
an agent of nature.
                    September, it doesn't matter,
doesn't open hearts anymore, the earth just
hardens slowly.
                    He comes home, locks
himself in, hiding from a servant. How smoothly
the lock turns. It is probably
in on the conspiracy. He's crying. The tiny frame of the great
philosopher, the seventh continent, is trembling.
His vest. His starched collar.
Yellow cheeks. Brown frock coat.
All these dispensables tremble,
as if the bombs had already fallen
on Frankfurt. His solitude, hard-woven,
thin as Dutch linen, trembles.

FEVER

Poland like a dry fever on
the lips of an émigré. Poland,
a map pressed by the steam irons
of long-distance trains. Don't forget
the taste of the first strawberry,
rain, the scent of wet lindens
in the evening; heed the metallic sound
of curses; take notes on hatred,
the sheared coat of alienation;
remember what links and what divides.
A land of people so innocent that
they cannot be saved. A sheep praised by a lion
for its right conduct, a poet who always
suffers. Land without sting, confession
with no mortal sins. Be alone.
Listen to the song of an unchristened
blackbird. The raw scent of spring is
flowing, a cruel sign.

KIERKEGAARD ON HEGEL

Kierkegaard said of Hegel: He reminds me of someone
who builds an enormous castle but lives himself
in a storehouse next to the construction.
The mind, by the same token, dwells in
the modest quarters of the skull,
and those glorious states
which were promised us are covered
with spiderwebs, for the time being we should enjoy
a cramped cell in the jailhouse, a prisoner's song,
the good mood of a customs officer, the fist
of a cop. We live in longing. In our dreams,
locks and bolts open up. Who didn't find shelter
in the huge looks to the small. God
is the smallest poppy seed in the world,
bursting with greatness.

WE KNOW EVERYTHING

We know everything we read a lot
and despite our tender years our knees
have swabbed the floors of many churches
Battle or the boredom of a tight circle
awaits us a warm understanding or
the burden of belated adulthood
We will drink because one
drinks we'll walk unshaven
in shabby coats with hands
in our pockets because the twentieth century
is not the Golden Age rather its manly hand
has an iron grip
We will retreat we'll be sheltered
by the lie which always bides its time
and by the smallness of necessary habits
The mind will once more waken
a pungent taste of thoughts so
it is still an open question whether we'll grow
into Catholics or into Christians.

IN THE TREES

In the trees, in the crowns of the trees, under rich
robes of leaves, under cassocks of splendor,
under the senses, under wings, under wands,
a peaceful, sleepy life is hiding in the trees,
it breathes, it circles, a sketch of eternity.
Kingdoms of plenty gather in the lecterns
of the oaks. Squirrels are running, motionless
as the little russet sunsets hidden
under eyelids. Invisible hostages
swarm under the husks of acorns.
Slaves bring in baskets of fruit and silver,
camels sway like an Arab scholar
over a manuscript, wells drink
water and vinegar, sour Europe
drips like the resins from cut wood. Vermeer paints
robes and a light that doesn't subside.
Thrushes are dancing under the circus tents.
Słowacki has moved to Paris already; he buys
and sells stocks fervently. A rich man
squeezes through a needle's eye,
he groans and moans, oh what pangs. Socrates
explains to prospectors of gold what
the lie is, what is right, what is virtue.
Oarsmen row slowly. Sailors sail
slowly. The survivors of the Warsaw
Uprising are drinking sweet tea. Their laundry
dries on the branches. Where is my country,
somebody asks in sleep. A green schooner
lies at rusty anchor. A choir of immortal
souls rehearses Bach cantatas, in complete silence.
Nearby, Captain Nemo takes his nap

on a narrow couch. A woodpecker cables
an urgent report on the capture of
Carthage and on the Boston Tea Party.
A weasel has no intention of changing
into Lady Macbeth, in the crowns of the trees
there are no qualms of conscience. Icarus
drowns serenely. God rewinds the reel. Punitive
expeditions return to the barracks. We shall live
long in the lines of an arabesque, in the hooting
of a tawny owl, in desires, in the echo which is
homeless, under rich robes of leaves,
in the crowns of the trees, in somebody's breath.

A RIVER

Poems from poems, songs
from songs, paintings from paintings,
always this friendly
impregnation. On the other bank
of the river, within range of being,
soldiers are marching. A black army,
a red army, a green army,
the iron rainbow. In between, smooth
water, an indifferent wave.

HE ACTS

He acts, in splendor and in darkness,
in the roar of waterfalls and in the silence of sleep,
but not as your well-protected shepherds
would have it. He looks for the longest line,
the road so circuitous
it is barely visible, and fades away
in suffering. Only blind men, only
owls feel sometimes its dwindling trace
under their eyelids.

LIFE SENTENCE

Those sufferings are over.
No crying anymore. In an old album
you look at the face of a Jewish child
fifteen minutes before it dies.
Your eyes are dry. You put the kettle on,
drink tea, eat an apple.
You'll live.

ODE TO PLURALITY

I don't understand it all and I am
even glad that the world like a restless
ocean exceeds my ability
to understand the essence of water, rain,
of plunging into Baker's Pond, near
the Bohemian-German border, in
September 1980, a detail without any special
meaning, the deep Germanic pond.
Let the half-oxidized ego breathe
steadily, let the swimmer cross the
meridian, it's evening, owls wake up
from their daily sleep, far away
cars whir lazily. Who once
touched philosophy is lost
and won't be saved by a poem, there is
always the rest, difficult to reckon,
a soreness. Who once learned a wild
run of poetry will not taste anymore
the stony calm of family narratives
whose every chapter is the nest
of a single generation. Who once lived won't
forget the changing delight of seasons,
he will dream even of nettles and burdocks, and the
spiders in his dream won't look any worse
than swallows. Who has once met
irony will burst into laughter
during the prophet's lecture. Who once prayed
with more than just a dry mouth
will remember the presence of the strange echo
coming from a wall. Who once
was silent would rather not talk

over dessert. And who was struck
by the shock of love will return to his books
with an altered face.
You, singular soul, stand before
this abundance. Two eyes, two hands,
ten inventive fingers, and
only one ego, the wedge of an orange,
the youngest of sisters. And the pleasure of
hearing doesn't destroy the pleasure of
seeing, though that flurry of freedom disturbs
the peace of the other gentle senses.
Peace, thick nothing, as full of sweet
juice as a pear in September.
Brief moments of happiness vanish
under an avalanche of oxygen, in winter
a lonely rook strikes his beak against the white
surface of the lake, another time
a couple of woodpeckers, scared
by an ax, are looking outside my window
for a poplar that is sick enough.
An absent woman writes long
letters and yearning swells like
opium; in an Egyptian museum,
the same yearning, unshaken and unbroken,
rubbed into a brown papyrus a few thousand years
older. Love letters always end up
in museums, the curious are
more persistent than lovers.
Ego gulps air, reason awakens
from its daily sleep, the swimmer gets out
of the water. A beautiful woman plays
a happy one, men pretend they are braver
than they really are, the Egyptian
museum doesn't hide human weaknesses.
To live, if only to live longer,

giving oneself perhaps to the power
of one of the colder stars and mocking it
sometimes because it is slimy and cool
like a frog in a pond. A poem grows
on contradiction but it can't cover it.

GOOD FRIDAY IN THE TUNNELS OF THE MÉTRO

Jews of various religions meet
in the tunnels of the Métro, rosary beads
spilled from someone's tender fingers.

Above them priests sleep after their Lenten supper,
above them the pyramids of synagogues and churches
stand like the rocks a glacier left behind.

I listened to the *St. Matthew Passion*,
which transforms pain into beauty.
I read the *Death Fugue* by Celan
transforming pain into beauty.

In the tunnels of the Métro no transformation of pain,
it is there, it persists and is keen.

VAN GOGH'S FACE

Noon, streams of the melting crowd,
Paris. On a kiosk, a draft
notice for a new graduation class extorted
from the registry of births
next to ads for fox furs and Beaujolais nouveau.
Among them appears your clear-cut face, the face
of a just man, anxiety
dressed in skin.
We disperse, we pass by, we swim
under the blade of that excruciating look.
And you watch us, rich man,
more alive than living ones and more
collected.

IN MAY

As I walked at dawn in the forest,
in May, I kept asking where you are, souls
of the dead. Where are you, the young ones
who are missing, where are you,
the completely transformed?
Great stillness reigned in the forest,
and I heard the green leaves dream,
I heard the dream of the bark from which
boats, ships, and sails will arise.
Then, slowly, birds joined in,
goldfinches, thrushes, blackbirds
on the balconies of branches, each of them spoke
differently, in his own voice, not asking for anything,
with no bitterness or regret.
And I realized you are in singing,
unseizable as music, indifferent as
musical notes, distant from us
as we are from ourselves.

FIRE

Probably I am an ordinary middle-class
believer in individual rights, the word
"freedom" is simple to me, it doesn't mean
the freedom of any class in particular.
Politically naïve, with an average
education (brief moments of clear vision
are its main nourishment), I remember
the blazing appeal of that fire which parches
the lips of the thirsty crowd and burns
books and chars the skin of cities. I used to sing
those songs and I know how great it is
to run with others; later, by myself,
with the taste of ashes in my mouth, I heard
the lie's ironic voice and the choir screaming
and when I touched my head I could feel
the arched skull of my country, its hard edge.

FIRE, FIRE

The fire of Descartes, the fire of Pascal,
the ash, the sparkle.
At night, an invisible bonfire blazes,
the fire which, burning, doesn't destroy
but creates, as if it wanted to restore
in one moment all that was ravished
by flames on various continents—
the library at Alexandria, the faith
of the Romans, and the fear of a small girl
somewhere in New Zealand.
                          The fire, like armies
of Mongols, ravages and burns cities
made of wood, of stone, but later it erects
airy houses and unseen palaces,
it compels Descartes
to overthrow philosophy and to build up a new one,
it transforms itself into the burning bush,
awakens Pascal, sets bells pealing
and melts them with its abundant zeal.
Have you seen how it reads
books? Page after page, slowly,
like someone who has just learned
how to spell.
                  Fire, fire, eternal
fire of Heraclitus, a rapacious messenger,
a boy with a mouth stained by blackberries.

THE SELF

It is small and no more visible than a cricket
in August. It likes to dress up, to masquerade,
as all dwarfs do. It lodges between
granite blocks, between serviceable
truths. It even fits under
a bandage, under adhesive. Neither customs officers
nor their beautiful dogs will find it. Between
hymns, between alliances, it hides itself.
It camps in the Rocky Mountains of the skull.
An eternal refugee. It is I and I,
with the fearful hope that I have found at last
a friend, am it. But the self
is so lonely, so distrustful, it does not
accept anyone, even me.
It clings to historical events
no less tightly than water to a glass.
It could fill a Neolithic jar.
It is insatiable, it wants to flow
in aqueducts, it thirsts for newer and newer vessels.
It wants to taste space without walls,
diffuse itself, diffuse itself. Then it fades away
like desire, and in the silence of an August
night you hear only crickets patiently
conversing with the stars.

LIGHTNING

For Adam Michnik

We lived understanding little and craving
knowledge. As plants do, when they grow toward
light, we sought justice
and we found it only in the plants,
in the leaves of the horse chestnut, enormous
as oblivion, in the fern shrubs which swayed
slowly and made no promises.
In silence. In music. In a poem. We sought
justice, confusing it with beauty.
Emotion is governed by strict laws.
We turned our backs on cruelty
and boredom. There's no solution, that much
we knew, there are only fragments, and the fact that
we spoke in complete sentences seemed to us
a strange joke. How easy it was to hate
a policeman. Even his face seemed to us
a part of his uniform. The errors of others
were easy to detect. On a hot day, the river
reflected mountains, clouds. Life then was
round like a balloon when it gets going.
Spruces stood still, filled with shadows
and stillness like the depths of an ocean. Green
eyes, your wet skin,
my lizard. In the evening, mute lightning
flickered in the sky. It was other people's thoughts
burning down safety. One had to
pack in a hurry and go farther,
east or west, mapping out
an escape route.

A VIEW OF DELFT

Houses, waves, clouds, and shadows
(deep-blue roofs, brownish bricks),
all of you finally became a glance.

The quiet pupil of things, unreined,
glittering with blackness.

You'll outlive our admiration, our tears,
and our noisy, despicable wars.

TO . . .

Madam Death, I am writing to request
that you kindly take into consideration
an extension of my liability to
the institution headed by you
for so many centuries. You, Madam,
are a master, a violent sport,
a delicate ax, the pope, velvet lips,
scissors. I don't flatter you. I beg.
I don't demand. In my defense I have
only silence, dew on the grass, a nightingale
among the branches. You forgive it,
its long tenure in the leaves of one aspen
after another, drops of eternity, grams
of amazement, and the sleepy complaints of the poor poets
whose passports you didn't renew.

IT COMES TO A STANDSTILL

The city comes to a standstill
and life turns into still life,
it is as brittle as plants in a herbarium.
You ride a bicycle which doesn't
move, only the houses wheel by,
slowly, showing their noses, brows,
and pouting lips. The evening becomes
a still life, it doesn't feel like existing,
therefore it glistens like a Chinese lantern
in a peaceful garden. Nightfall, motionless,
the last one. The last word. Happiness
hovers in the crowns of the trees.
Inside the leaves, kings are asleep.
No word, the yellow sail of the sun
towers over the roofs like a tent abandoned
by Caesar. Pain becomes a still life and despair
is only a still life, framed
by the mouth of one passerby. The square
keeps silent in a dark foliage of birds'
wings. Silence as on the fields of Jena
after the battle when loving women
look at the faces of the slain.

IN THE PAST

In the past, we had faith in invisible
things, in shadows and their shadows,
in light—dark and pink as an eyelid.
Ah, the jaws of a camera bite images.
So now we can believe only
in the past, just as the poor past
used to believe in us, his great-grandchildren.
He dreamed that we could escape
from the trap which in every generation was set
by Danton and Robespierre, Beria and the other
ambitious disciples. Because there is no refuge,
there is refuge. Because invisible things
exist together with sounds
that no one hears. There is no consolation
and there is consolation, under
the elbow of desire, where pearls
would grow, if only tears had memories.
And yet a skater doesn't lose his balance
pushing back from the precipice. And the
dawn and the milkman get up early
and run through snow, leaving white traces,
soon filled with water. A small bird
drinks that water and it sings and once more
it saves the disorder of things and you and me
and the singing.

THE DARK GOD, THE LIGHT GOD

The Dark One in lightning,
the Light One at midnight
when the stars grow dim in his splendor

Child who plays with the ocean
and builds up cathedrals of waves, salty stained glass

The Dark God of blasphemy, the true one,
like the prayer of an old monk
who is no more a man
than a woman

Great rains of weeping and the wall of joy

The God of slavery, docile giant,
tamed member of the household
Cruel God, slayer of children

Infinite background that imprisons
and pierces us, incomparable background
flaring in the night like a match

The Dark God of cursing, the Light
God who lives in an apple, in bread

DON'T ALLOW THE LUCID MOMENT
TO DISSOLVE

Don't allow the lucid moment to dissolve
Let the radiant thought last in stillness
though the page is almost filled and the flame flickers
We haven't risen yet to the level of ourselves
Knowledge grows slowly like a wisdom tooth
The stature of a man is still notched
high up on a white door
From far off, the joyful voice of a trumpet
and of a song rolled up like a cat
What passes doesn't fall into a void
A stoker is still feeding coal into the fire
Don't allow the lucid moment to dissolve
On a hard dry substance
you have to engrave the truth

THAT FORCE

The force that pulses
in the boughs of trees
and in the sap of plants
also inhabits poems
but it's calm there

The force that hovers
in a kiss and in desire
lies also in poems
though it is hushed

The force that grows
in Napoleon's dreams
and tells him to conquer Russia and snow
is also in poems
but is very still.

SONG OF AN EMIGRÉ

We come into being in alien cities.
We call them native but not for long.
We are allowed to admire their walls and spires.
From east to west we go, and in front of us
rolls the huge circle of a flaming
sun through which, nimbly, as in a circus,
a tamed lion jumps. In alien cities
we look at the work of Old Masters
and we recognize our faces in the old
paintings without surprise. We lived
before and we even knew suffering,
we lacked only words. At the Orthodox
church in Paris, the last White
gray-haired Russians pray to God, who
is centuries younger than they and equally
helpless. In alien cities we'll
remain, like trees, like stones.

Yes, my life was short, yes, I loved,
felt a light growing, yes, under
my fingers sparks were born.
Yes, I had little time, I didn't know
how much, I pitied Gretchen,
dead youth, the unrequited.
No, the flame wasn't mute, yes,
I ran through icy forests,
chased by snow, yellow stars,
and by the strangeness of style itself; no, not the police,
I don't know if it was a devil. There was no epoch, only
green grass, ash trees, becalmed
objects, dragonflies over ponds,
but no epoch, a wooden floor,
reticent chairs, yes, Vienna,
the taste of coffee, same as now,
pigeons on the windowsills. No, I didn't
foresee the Spring Tide of Nations,
I don't know, don't remember, this question
is too personal. No, I'm not
familiar with Wagner's music. Can we
communicate? Regret, even envy,
I don't know whether it's fate, a glove,
such delicate snowflakes, if only
they don't turn into a blizzard.
The green eyes of that girl.
My destiny was too big, like a tent,
my heart throbbed so clumsily
in those huge rooms, yes, talent,
teeth crushing bitter coffee beans.
No, I was afraid, I was surrounded on all sides,

the armies of mercenaries charged, straight at me,
ah, gentlemen, how could you
compare me to Admiral Nelson,
no, shadows bellowed, whispers
pealed like cathedral bells, appearances
barked, yes, I admit I was wrong
sometimes, how could I know
that I was Schubert? I was in the state
of becoming, looked for a way, a color,
you can't know me; only an echo.
Yes, I was in that strait where
suffering changes into song,
yes, evergreen forests and unrequited love,
the joy of being indifferent, precisely
I wanted to say, the happiness
of expression, halfway
between life and death,
exactly halfway, yes, even here
the cheers of dancing people reach us,
but they clot in the gelatin of memory.
Don't turn back, don't take the wrong direction,
but of course you can't transform life
into a Lied, it's only a very small Noah's Ark,
you know, gentlemen, not people but
species, not flowers but specimens,
not fragrances but descriptions. While we ran
wild in the meadow's luxury,
in weeds and in wind, in dandelions and anemones,
in the huge plural of sounds and colors,
passionate and speechless, submissive to the demands
of breathless messengers, in jubilation,
in sin, in prayer, morning
and evening, in boredom and laughter,
that eternal dance lasted, May, June,
so many things were happening, fear and games,

cut fingers, gaping mouth,
real kisses and kisses only
in daydreams, braids, ears of wheat,
your glances, a veranda, silence,
and nothing, the crimson of the fall, yes, I remember
everything, larks on long threads,
poppies, a hazel grove, the warm brick of the city,
the voices fading in the dusk, and night—
a box in which children hide
their treasures, the sleep and the vigil, Venus
in the pale sky shivering from cold.
Yes, it is even better now, only two lips
talk to themselves in the singing,
a piano nearby in its gleaming tuxedo.
Yes, I am tired now, and no, it's not
a complaint.

ESCALATOR

How motionless they stand on moving stairs,
the statues of my unknown neighbors.
How slowly they ascend, without effort
or exhaustion. Beneath them lies a city
which will not be conquered now,
since no one lays sieges these days.
Fate capitulates with pleasure,
and the victors are no worse than those before them.

The sun descends the same as always,
a horizon brushed with rosy cream.
The streets lie open as empty beer cans,
they sing the same song unbidden.
Why should the cities be vanquished,
why hurl stones and ravage shrines,
when scorn, whispers, and laughter will suffice.
The stairs rise like pine forests.

St. Bartholomew's Night may last for fifteen minutes,
bloodless—only courage corrodes slowly.
I watch the crowd as it moves upwards.
So many faces, so many cheeks,
such hope, anticipation, hands clasped,
in the irises of convex eyes
light crisscrosses shadows.

So many faces, so many palms,
and only one imagination.
Those of us returning know already:
nothing waits for us above.
Pigeons battle over scraps of bread,

with swift hieroglyphics the swallows
write letters to the president,
and the president laughs like the wind.

—tr. Clare Cavanagh

THERE WILL BE A FUTURE

There will be rain, there will be feasts, there
will be bonfires, chestnut husks will crack,
there will be shouts, someone will hide in the bushes,
someone will trip over a cherrystone,
a smell of gas and lilacs in the air.
There will be laughter, there will be cries, prayers, demure
and silent lies, there will be a future,
only you will stay here, in this second-
class waiting room at the railroad station, dark with
cigar smoke, under the portrait of the Austrian Emperor.

WITHOUT END

Also in death we are going to live,
only in a different way, delicately, softly,
dissolved in music;
one by one called out to the corridor,
lonely and yet in a group,
like schoolmates from the same class
which extends beyond the Ural Mountains
and reaches the Quaternary. Released
from unending conversation on politics,
open and candid, at ease, even though
shutters are being closed with a bang
and hail will rattle on the windowsill
its Turkish march, dashing,
as usual. The world of appearances won't fade away
at once, for a long time it will continue
to grumble and curl like a wet
page thrown into the fire. The quest for perfection
will find fulfillment casually, it will bypass
all obstacles just as the Germans
learned how to bypass the Maginot Line. Paltry
things, forgotten, kites made of the thinnest
paper, brittle leaves from past autumns,
will recover their immortal dignity and the systems,
big and victorious, will wither like a giant's sex.
No longing anymore. It will overtake
itself, amazed that it chased for so long
its arctic shadow. And we will be no more,
not having learned yet
how to live at such an altitude.

IN THE ENCYCLOPEDIAS,
NO ROOM FOR OSIP MANDELSTAM

In the encyclopedias once again no room for
Osip Mandelstam again he is
homeless still it's so difficult to find a flat
How to register in Moscow it's nearly impossible
The Caucasus still calls him Asia's lowland forest
roars these days haven't arrived yet
Someone else picks up pebbles on the Black Sea beaches
This shifting investigation goes on though the uniform
is of a new cut and its wooden-headed tailor
almost fell over bowing
You close a book it sounds like a gunshot
White dust from the paper tickles your nose a Latin
evening is here it snows nobody will come tonight
it's bedtime but if he knocks at your thin door
let him in

THE GENERATION

To the memory of Helmut Kajzar

We walked very slowly down the concrete
slabs near the Olympic Stadium
in Berlin, where the black star
of Jesse Owens had flamed in that prehistoric
time, and the German air
had screamed. I wanted to laugh,
I couldn't believe you could walk
so slowly in the place he had run so fast;
to walk in one direction, but to look
in another, like the figures in Egyptian
reliefs. And yet we were walking that
way, bound with the light string
of friendship.
Two kinds of deaths circle about us.
One puts our whole group to sleep,
takes all of us, the whole herd.
Later it makes long speeches to substantiate
the sentence. The other one is wild, illiterate,
it catches us alone, strayed,
we animals, we bodies, we the pain,
we careless and uneducated.
We worship both of them in two religions
broken by schism. That scar
divided us sometimes when I had
forgotten: we have two deaths,
and one life.
Don't look back when you hear
my whisper. In the huge crowd of Greeks,
Egyptians, and Jews, in that fertile

generation turned to ashes, you walk straight
ahead, as then, unhurried,
alone.
The walls are not tight, windows open
at night to the rain, to the songs of stars
muffled by distance. But
every moment lasts eternally, becomes
a point, a haven, an envelope of emotion.
Every thought is a light coin which
rolls, in its shy secretive
being, into a song, into a painting. Every joy,
even the nonexistent one, leaves a transparent trace. Frost
kisses the pane because it can't get into the room.
This is how a new country arises,
built by us as if by mere chance,
constructed for the future, going down, in tunnels,
the bright shadow of the first country, an unfinished
house.

THREE VOICES

The cloud of dusk gathers in the room.
The shadows of night are growing, tamed desire.
On the radio, Mahler's *Song of the Earth*.
Outside the window, blackbirds whistle, carefree and loud.
And I can hear the soft rustling
of my blood (as if snow were sliding down the mountains).
These three voices, these three alien voices,
are speaking to me but they don't
demand anything, they make no promise.
In the background, somewhere
in the meadow, the cortege of night,
full of hollow whispers, forms
and re-forms, trying to get in order.

ESPRIT D'ESCALIER

On a staircase as cheerless
as a camera obscura, in a zoo inhabited
by letters, mice, and flies, the blue spark
of thought flares up suddenly. High above,
a tumultuous party is in progress,
a noisy festival in the plural. The night,
a nun in a broad-rimmed
bonnet, runs down St. John's
Street. Shy words,
unspoken before, emerge,
the word "yes," the word "no," an expression of scorn,
an exhibition of logic: finally, breathless,
like a sprinter, the triumphant
discourse appears. It comes accompanied by
shadows, phantasms, insolvent dreams,
a first kiss with the huge
figure *1* flashing across the sky,
a high school prom, funny tunes,
You are my destiny, and, sure enough,
what happens bears a striking resemblance
to destiny, the same eyes, the same
nose, though the meaning is totally
different. Parades march down the street
under an ever-newer banner,
in apartments husbands kill
the youth of their wives, on the staircase,
in semi-darkness, among half-opened
windows, drafts, partial
handrails, and landings, a different
realm spreads out. Dimness is
simply a lack of light, a darker

shadow, crumpled paper, grayer
grayness, black whiteness, dead
carmine. Dimness emboldens letters, mice,
and flies, you hear light steps
and faint echoes, on the windowsill
the tired leaflets are dozing,
daughters of pathos and gossip. Invisible,
wedged under a threshold, a spider,
the quasi-god of that region, weaves
its gluey web. The flies are not
convinced of its existence, they
merely laugh, shed a tear sometimes, or
a silent prayer. Uncollected,
orphaned, the letters read
their obscure messages slowly
as in a geology textbook,
stamps unstick from envelopes.
On a wall, close to a cellar,
a slogan scribbled crookedly
with chalk: *There is nothing worse than
someone else's ego*, and an illegible signature,
a C maybe, or a Z.
It's enough to reach out your hand
and right away a back yard begins,
empty now, like a saucer waiting
for strawberries, turtledoves
sleep watchfully, they will be retained
in the preserve of the local children's
memory. Objects whisper to each other,
old wood creaks.
One of the oldest mice
is named Voltaire and is stubbornly
taciturn, he despises the Romantic period,
even after death he avoids speaking
of death. Who praises the night at night

won't live till dawn. The lure of
darkness, sweet like milk
chocolate, doesn't make sense and
the old mouse in the wig makes a face.
Up above, the party and the clatter
continue, in a moment someone in a halo
of joy will leave the company, will fall
heavily on the pavement, will take
a French leave, will flow like oxygen, will sail
looking in memory for
the unspoken words which, like
lead sewn into linen, will pull him
down, into grass, reeds, sand,
mud. But in the gray, restrained
world of the stairs, after a hollow moment
of dread, love moans will sound again,
and fierce altercations, and ironic sighings.

IN THE BEAUTY CREATED BY OTHERS

Only in the beauty created
by others is there consolation,
in the music of others and in others' poems.
Only others save us,
even though solitude tastes like
opium. The others are not hell,
if you see them early, with their
foreheads pure, cleansed by dreams.
That is why I wonder what
word should be used, "he" or "you." Every "he"
is a betrayal of a certain "you" but
in return someone else's poem
offers the fidelity of a sober dialogue.

OVER AMERICA

The airplane flies through the storm, a mobile
lightning rod. An umbrella. A waiting room
in the act of displacement. Yesterday
a certain American professor spoke
on Różewicz (led to slaughter
he survived). Lightning cut the sky
like nimble razor blades (no one's thoughts).
He survived, we survived.
                                        Life is so
gluey and lazy, but death has an enormous
sense of form, it was not for nothing
that he sat for hours in Rembrandt's studio,
a watchman in black, a shadow standby.
The cabin attendant smiles like
the Statue of Liberty (or rather,
the Statue of Courtesy).
                                        Among heavy
clouds, through ink, brocade,
the plane searches for the route to the airport.
To survive means to be in storm,
on a ship which plunges among electric
thoughts, to be in the wax of the body
in its first or last form. Again,
and lightly, my unfaithful mute ego flies
above the stairs. There is no end
to the steps of initiation. The cool
brass of the last door handle
won't touch the forehead as long as
the bird's Amen
does not resound.

IRON

Why it has to be December.
The dark doves of snow fly,
falling on the slabs of the sidewalk. What is
talent against iron, what is
thought against a uniform, what is music
against a truncheon, what is joy against
fear, the dark heavy snow encloses
the sprouts of the dream, from a balcony you notice
as young Norwid shows his I.D.
to the police and he pleads
he cannot sign the volkslist, the patrolmen
laugh with contempt, they have snorting
nostrils and red-hot cheeks,
tormentors hired from the scenes
of the Passion, what's that silent crowd
in a blue streetcar against them,
who's that sad girl, is that the way
the new epoch begins, is this tank
with a long Gogolian nose its godfather,
and that gritting iron weighing down
the delicate dove of snow,
will it seal the Declaration
of Loyalty and mortally wound
the freedom song, meanwhile you notice
as young Norwid, released by
the snorting nostrils and blood-red
cheeks, is hiding in a gateway, he,
exactly like you, is as breakable
as a record, and
the passersby—each of them carrying a handful
of infinity—all

are rounded up, all are frozen,
the cobblestone wavers under the tank treads
of decrees. At night you ask me,
desperate, what to do; why, I wonder,
has your concept proven false
or the hoop of your imagination snapped, no,
only iron has swollen.

PALM SUNDAY

For U.

Christ crucified at daybreak,
a week too early, unshaven,
in soiled clothes, with a grimace
of bewilderment on his skinny face,
surrounded by soldiers
in half-buttoned uniforms,
nailed to the wood in haste.
The exaltations of the Week called off,
murky Wednesday and the hatred of Friday.
They discontinued the retreat
and the mystical ascent
of adolescent boys, we've lost our chance for
the seven ascetic days, there's no time
for penance, new feasts are forthcoming,
full of the unknown triumphs of fire.

READING BOOKS

Reading books, ah, we kept forgetting
who wrote them and what fights there were
on every page, in every sentence.
The dark moving wood, as on a stage,
grew around the pen, an arrow snatched
in flight, a quill stolen
from half-real birds. It's only now
they stand still on the bookshelves, so incurious
without recollection, like old men warming themselves
on a street bench in the sun.
Reading books, we kept forgetting
that fear is a wolf who dreads himself
at nightfall and doesn't know if
there is a mirror someplace, or a spring,
able to put out the yellow flicker
in his slanted eyes. We read books
in order to learn, with relief,
how dangerous Plato's beast is, the drowsy
tiger that kills only in daylight.

POEMS ON POLAND

I read poems on Poland written
by foreign poets. Germans and Russians
have not only guns, but also
ink, pens, some heart, and a lot
of imagination. Poland in their poems
reminds me of an audacious unicorn
which feeds on the wool of tapestries, it is
beautiful, weak, and imprudent. I don't know
what the mechanism of illusion is based on,
but even I, a sober reader,
am enraptured by that fairy-tale defenseless land
on which feed black eagles, hungry
emperors, the Third Reich, and the Third Rome.

CITY UNKNOWN

O unknown city, cool cradle
Snow falling on a map

The tenements' green roofs
The windowsills where laughter rattles

Unknown city hidden away among
I don't know how many gentle hills

What was ordinary isn't possible anymore
A different wind turns the tin vane

In the imperial forest in the royal pantry
wild cherries waited so sweet and black
one could feed them to Leviathan

And fate gave into our hands the blood-filled
Star of Bethlehem whittled with a knife

THE TRIAL

One prosecutor (bald, speaks in low voice,
stammering), three judges (that one
on the right plays with the glasses
belonging to the one who sits
in the middle), three bearded defendants
(exchanging smiles with the audience),
three attorneys (white hair, memo books,
gowns hemmed with a thin stripe of green),
three lies, two semi-truths, one
justice (nonattendant, without excuse),
outside the window a rook polishes its eternal gown.
The woman clerk yawns. The judge, that one who
sits on the left, counts nonexistent
trees on a dusty wall. Boredom
rhymes with itself, as if it were
a physical person. The prosecutor lashes
the memory of the defendants, what does it mean
in the face of oblivion, whose being
the court has forgotten. Someone weeps and some stifled
reality, pale like the shoots of winter
potatoes, germinates again.
The judge, a tailor with the qualities of a demiurge,
still ponders openly and secretly
how many years he'll cut down his own and those three lives,
the common divine rosy fire-resistant life.

MY MASTERS

My masters are not infallible.
They're neither Goethe,
who had a sleepless night
only when distant volcanoes moaned, nor Horace,
who wrote in the language of gods
and altar boys. My masters
seek my advice. In fleecy
overcoats hurriedly slipped on
over their dreams, at dawn, when
the cool wind interrogates the birds,
my masters talk in whispers.
I can hear their broken speech.

SAD, TIRED

Sad, tired, lonely, and not pretty,
You stand by the window, next to the canvas
Called the street, the world, or the city,
Madame Arnolfini cut off from her husband.
Bergson's insect sways, sways
Trapped in the spiderweb. Between us,
Oceans flow. Between us, cyclones
Sleep. Between us, wars slumber.
The alienation of others wears on. Between us,
Generals count arrows in a quiver.
Between us, yearning blazes. Sad,
Tired, not pretty, and lonely, please forbear,
Open wide the white fan of the window.

YOUR TELEPHONE CALL

Your telephone call broke in
while I was writing a letter to you.
Do not disturb me when
I'm talking with you. Our two
absences cross,
and one love rips itself apart
like a bandage.

THIS

This that lies heavy
and weighs down,
that aches like ache
and burns like a slap in the face,
is a stone
or an anchor.

A VIEW OF KRAKOW

Before me, Krakow in a gray valley.
Swallows bear it on long braids
of air. Rooks in black cloaks
look after it. Hungry bees
buzz in the bird-cherry bushes.
Cats on the roofs of cars keep watch.
What was, what is, are carefully divided.
Kings in marble tombs, tombs
in crypts, God in prayers, fingers
in rings.
Before me, the Church of St. Catherine,
never finished (like a rough
draft). Gothic arches trudge
upwards, the shoulderblades of sleepy monks
who've forgotten which word
wakes the Lord. A low valley before me.
A lonely old woman lived
here and died not long ago of age
or loneliness. Who will remember
the kind of dough she baked, her
angry eyes? Which nation
claims her now? Who granted her asylum?
(A tattered passport, eyes: brazen.)
Black poplars stand beside her
and a nightingale trapped in the leaves rehearses,
as always, its pearly prophecy.
In the evening the bats' uncertain flight
builds fragile covenants.
Before me Krakow, a gray valley.
A girl runs, late for her lecture,

through a dense tunnel of trees.
Petals of peonies grow in her hair,
time's tenderness weaves a nest in her hair.
She runs fast, but she doesn't move,
she's always in the same spot,
beneath the chestnuts, which cast off old greenery
and put on new.
Before me, gleaming grass, open
penknives, starlings like scouts, the horizon,
other cities, borders, balconies, thoughts,
double meanings. Mists rise
and fall. The great bodies of churches
sway slowly like captive
balloons, their bells, proud, bronze
hearts, emit spidery sounds.
Children run across the flagstones
trundling hoops, and the sun ahead of them,
craving coolness, hides in the shade
of sycamores. Chimneys send up thin smoke trails,
as if conclaves were always in session
and as if even the apartment buildings longed
to join in the game of existence
and I hear the song, ever louder,
growing in the courtyards' wolfish throats,
song of the forgotten, song of the wronged,
the mute, the absent, the dead,
the voices of those who passed quietly through life,
I hear, I hear the rising music,
racket, roar, prayer, lullaby,
the song of drowning ships, the cries of the survivors.
In the morning orioles ask for water, in the evening
owls weep and jilted sweethearts
fret in the local theater
and a wild song vibrates in so many larynxes

and the prisoner and the secret policeman nod off as does the
    everlasting
world borrowed from a great library.

—tr. Clare Cavanagh

MOMENT

Clear moments are so short.
There is much more darkness. More
ocean than terra firma. More
shadow than form.

FROM

CANVAS

(1991)

TRANSLATED BY RENATA GORCZYNSKI,

BENJAMIN IVRY, AND C. K. WILLIAMS

LULLABY

No sleep, not tonight. The window blazes.
Over the city, fireworks soar and explode.
No sleep: too much has gone on.
Rows of books stand vigil above you.
You'll brood on what's happened
and what hasn't. No sleep, not tonight.
Your inflamed eyelids will rebel,
your fiery eyes sting,
your heart swell with remembrance.
No sleep. The encyclopedias will open
and poets, dressed carefully,
bundled for winter, will stroll out one by one.
Memory will open, with a sudden hiss
like a parachute's. Memory will open,
you won't sleep,
rocked slowly through clouds,
an easy target in the fireworks' glow.
No sleep: so much has gone on,
so much been revealed.
You know each drop of blood
could compose its own scarlet *Iliad*,
each dawn author
a dark diary. No sleep,
under the thick blanket of roofs, attics,
and chimneys casting out handfuls of ash.
Pale nights row noiselessly into the sky,
their oars silk stockings delicately rustling.
You'll go out to the park, and tree limbs
will amiably thump your shoulder, making
sure, confirming your fidelity. No sleep.
You'll race through the uninhabited park,

a shadow facing more shadows.
You'll think of someone who's no more
and of someone else living so fully
that her life at its edges changes
to love. Light, more light
gathers in the room. No sleep, not tonight.

ANECDOTE OF RAIN

I was strolling under the tents of trees
and raindrops occasionally reached me
as though asking:
Is your desire to suffer,
to sob?

Soft air,
wet leaves;
—the scent was spring, the scent sorrow.

LAVA

And what if Heraclitus and Parmenides
are both right
and two worlds exist side by side,
one serene, the other insane; one arrow
thoughtlessly hurtles, another, indulgent,
looks on; the selfsame wave moves and stands still.
Animals all at once come into the world
and leave it, birch leaves dance in the wind
as they fall apart in the cruel, rusty flame.
Lava kills and preserves, the heart beats
and is beaten; there was war, then there wasn't;
Jews died, Jews stay alive, cities are razed,
cities endure, love fades, the kiss everlasting,
the wings of the hawk must be brown,
you're still with me though we're no more,
ships sink, sand sings, clouds wander
like wedding veils in tatters.

All's lost. So much brilliance. The hills
gently descend with their long banners of woods.
Moss inches up the stone tower of a church,
its small mouth timidly praising the North.
At dusk, the savage lamp of the jasmine is glowing,
possessed by its own luminescence.
Before a dark canvas in a museum,
eyes narrow like a cat's. Everything's finished.
Riders gallop black horses, a tyrant composes
a sentence of death with grammatical errors.
Youth dissolves
in a day; girls' faces freeze
into medallions, despair turns to rapture

and the hard fruits of stars in the sky
ripen like grapes, and beauty endures, shaken, unperturbed,
and God is and God dies; night returns to us
in the evening, and the dawn is hoary with dew.

R. SAYS

Literary rats—says R.—that's us.
We meet on line at discount movies;
at dusk, when brocaded suns sink in green ponds,
we leave the libraries, fattened on Kafka.
Enlightened rats, in fatigues, or in the uniforms
of an army mustered by a literate despot;
the secret police of a poet who might be coming to power
at the edge of the city. Rats with stipends, confidential
grant applications, snide remarks; rats with slick hair
and meticulous whiskers.
Capitals, burning asphalt, philanthropic dowagers
all know us well, but not deserts, oceans, or jungles.
An atheist epoch's Benedictines, missionaries of easy despair,
we might be a link in an evolution
whose sense and address no one betrays.
We're compensated in small, worthless gold coin,
and with the moment of bliss when metaphor's flame
welds two free-floating objects, when a hawk lands,
or a tax inspector makes the sign of the cross.

INCORPOREAL RULER

Who owns the earth, you
ask, astonished. By day it's conquered
by square-skulled men:
police. At nights
we reclaim our homeland.
Who owns the leaves of the plane tree,
who tightens clock springs?
So many errors, with an incorporeal
ruler governing a tangible reality;
so many intermediaries, foxlike faces,
sly smiles, deceitful death.

A TALK WITH FRIEDRICH NIETZSCHE

Most highly respected Professor Nietzsche,
sometimes I seem to see you
on a sanatorium terrace at dawn
with fog descending and song bursting
the throats of the birds.

Not tall, head like a bullet,
you compose a new book
and a strange energy hovers around you.
Your thoughts parade
like enormous armies.

You know now that Anne Frank died,
and her classmates and friends, boys, girls,
and friends of her friends, and cousins
and friends of her cousins.

What are words, I want to ask you, what
is clarity and why do words keep burning
a century later, though the earth
weighs so much?

Clearly nothing links enlightenment
and the dark pain of cruelty.
At least two kingdoms exist,
if not more.

But if there's no God and no force
welds elements in repulsion,
then what are words really, and from whence
does their inner light come?

And from where does joy come, and where
does nothingness go? Where is forgiveness?
Why do the incidental dreams vanish at dawn
and the great ones keep growing?

SAILS

There were evenings, as scarlet as Phoenician sails,
that soaked up the light and the air; I was suddenly nearly gasping
for breath, blinded by the slanted rays
of the somnolent sun. This is how epochs end, I thought,
how overloaded ships sink, how the eyelids
of old theaters droop, and what's left is dust, smoke,
sharp stones underfoot, and fear looking like
joy, and the end, which is tranquillity.

Soon enough, though, it turns out to be only another
dress rehearsal, one more frantic improvisation:
the extras go home, swallows fall asleep
in precarious nests, the provincial
moon timidly slips into place,
robbers steal wigs, a priest writes to his mother.

How patiently you prepare and inure us,
what time you lavish on us,
what a teacher of history you are, Earth!

AT DAYBREAK

From the train window at daybreak,
I saw empty cities sleeping,
sprawled defenselessly on their backs
like great beasts.
Through the vast squares, only my thoughts
and a biting wind wandered;
linen flags fainted on towers,
birds started to wake in the trees,
and in the thick pelts of the parks
stray cats' eyes gleamed.
The shy light of morning, eternal
debutante, was reflected in shop windows.
Carousels, finally possessing themselves, spun
like prayer wheels on their invisible fulcrums;
gardens fumed like Warsaw's smoldering ruins.
The first van hadn't arrived yet
at the brown slaughterhouse wall.
Cities at daybreak are no one's,
and have no names.
And I, too, have no name,
dawn, the stars growing pale,
the train picking up speed.

THE CREATION OF THE WORLD

Mornings, curled asleep in our soft beds,
and in history, cruel, sluggish, dark rings
under its eyes, mint leaves on its so weary lids,
mornings, birds impatiently strut
on the sill and call us to action. Furious
doves who hid behind curtains shriek
in hollow Mozartean tones: It exists! It's being built,
in the meadow and forest and next to the pond
where the odor of dry willow hovers
and a lark bathes in a puddle.
Up, quick, the rooster's running,
leaned forward like a sprinter; dawn
blushes, owls depart without a goodbye,
the insurgent flag of the darkness is fading.
Again silence falls, the great performance
delays, again sleep, darkness, the void,
nothingness, lack of presence, its specific
slumbering pleasure. Now rain dictates
a long, tedious lecture and typewriters hidden
in garrets lazily clack
their humid spellings-out, slow, hesitant,
like a small nation's unconfident leader.
But now the rain falls silent, the gardens resume their chanting.
They sing from the depths of their brimming green hearts,
arbors and trees, the core of their leaves.
A blackbird appears in the void,
perfect, full of pride, as all living
creatures are proud of their endless warm
virtues. Dew scatters
on the grass, each hard drop
is a whole, closed in itself like a planet.

A grass snake is suddenly here, then a roe deer,
a reindeer, an ash, a black poplar. Evil contents itself
for the moment with its stinging trope of nettles.
Suddenly newer and newer fauna evolve,
and new countries, wars, short waves,
long waves, the ax, the gramophone record.
Trolleys ring their great school bell
for a recess. Clouds swim on their backs,
gazing calmly at the sun. At last you awake
(though God made man first, really woman is older).
There'll be storms, abrupt dusks under leaden,
too heavy clouds; there'll be hail, frozen tears,
long journeys in quiet trains,
but not every thunderbolt kills, not every death
means an ending, not every speech missing means silence.

MORANDI

Even at night, the objects kept vigil,
even as he slept, with African dreams;
a porcelain jug, two watering cans,
empty green wine bottles, a knife.
Even as he slept, deeply, as only creators
can sleep, dead-tired,
the objects were laughing, revolution was near.

The nosy watering can with its beak
feverishly incited the others;
blood pulsed wildly in the cup,
which had never known the thirst of a mouth,
only eyes, gazes, vision.

By day, they grew humble, and even took pride:
the whole coarse existence of the world
found refuge in them,
abandoning for a time the blossoming cherry,
the sorrowful hearts of the dying.

COVENANT

For Edward Hirsch

A moment of quiet covenant
in the Egyptian museum
in Turin; people and things, crowded
display cases, a German tour group's
noisy children, the watchful mummies,
annealed in the long fire of their contemplation,
lips tight as generals'
before battle;
the pyramids' granites, the statuettes
that protected the soul
from death and damnation,
until they were stolen
to serve no one again;
nail scissors
three thousand years old,
and my heart, as patient as a stammering
boy, and boisterous Italian families
loving their lives and their Sunday.
In proximity, shy,
without enmity, we were as one
and as one were aware of each other.
Time slipped like a copper pin
from the hair of a Pharaoh's daughter.
Blandly, amicably,
we watched one another, the old and young
of one world, mute and imperfect,
implements of desire and forgetting,
devices of pain and of love.
Even the polished knives that once could end longing
lay calmly on shelves, regretting perhaps
the tremor, the night plunge

in a breast, deception, dishonor.
Out the window, on the ocher-walled houses,
the sun rapidly wrote January's
festive proclamations.

PRESENCE

I was born in a city of wild cherries
and hard-seeded sunflowers (common wisdom
had it halfway from the West
to the East). Globes stained by verdigris
kept careless vigil.

Might only the absence of presence be perfect?
Presence, after all, infected with the original
sin of existence, is excessive, savage,
Oriental, superb, while beauty, like a fruit knife,
snips its bit of plentitude off.
Life accumulates through generations
as in a pond; it doesn't vanish
with its moment but turns
airy and dry. I think
of a half-conscious prayer, the chapped lips
of a boy at his first confession,
the wooden step creaking
under his knees.
At night, autumn arrives
for the harvest, yellow, ripe for flame.
There are, I know, not one
but at least four realities,
intersecting
like the Gospels.
I know I'm alone, but linked
firmly to you, painfully, gladly.
I know only the mysteries are immortal.

RUSSIA COMES INTO POLAND

For Joseph Brodsky

Through meadow and hedgerow, village and forest,
cavalries on the march, infantries on the march,
horses and cannons, old soldiers, young soldiers, children,
wiry wolfhounds at full gallop, a blizzard of feathers,
sleds, Black Marias, carriages, taxis,
even the old cars called Moskwitch come roaring in,
and warships and rafts and pontoon bridges roar in,
and barges, steamships, canoes (some of which sink),
barrage balloons, missiles, bombers,
howitzer shells whistling arias from an opera,
the shriek of flagellants and the growl of commands,
songs slashing the air with notes made of steel,
yurts and tents break camp, ropes tighten,
banners of dyed linen tremble overhead.
Messengers, panting, die as they run,
cables rush out, candles burning with quick crimson flames,
colonels dozing in carriages faster than light,
popes piously murmuring blessings,
even the moon is along on that hard, iron march.
Tanks, sabers, ropes,
Katyusha shells whirring like comets,
fifes and drums exploding the air,
clubs crunching, the heaving decks of ferries
and of invasions sigh, sway, the sons of the steppes
on the march, Moslems, condemned prisoners, lovers
of Byron, gamblers, the whole progeny
of Asia with Suvorov in the lead
limps in with a train of fawning courtiers who dance;
the yellow Volga runs in, Siberian rivers chanting,
camels pensively plod, bringing
the sands of the desert and humid mirages,

the fold-eyed Kirghizes marching in step,
the black pupils of the God of the Urals,
and behind them schoolteachers and languages straggle,
and behind them old manor houses skate in like gliders,
and German doctors with dressings and plasters;
the wounded with their alabaster faces,
regiments and divisions, cavalries, infantries, on the march,
Russia comes into Poland,
tearing cobwebs, leaves, silk ribbons,
ligaments and frontiers,
breaking
treaties, bridges, alliances,
threads, ties, clotheslines with wet washing still waving,
gates, arteries, bandages and conjunctions,
future and hope;
Russia comes in, marching
into a hamlet on the Pilica,
into the deep Mazovia forests,
rending posters and parliaments,
trampling roads, footbridges, paths, streams.
Russia comes into the eighteenth century,
into October, September, laughter and tears,
into conscience, into the concentration
of the student, the calm silence of the warm bricks of a wall,
comes into the fragrance
of meadows, herbs, the tangled paths of the forest,
trampling
the pansy, the wild rose,
hoofprints in the moss, tractor and tank prints
in the soft moss,
it overturns
chimneys, tree trunks, palaces,
turns off lights, makes great bonfires
out in the formal garden,
stains the clear spring,

razes the library, church, town hall,
flooding its scarlet banners through the sky,
Russia comes into my life,
Russia comes into my thought,
Russia comes into my poetry.

LATE FEAST

Evening, the edge of the city, a whole day
of void, then all at once
the late feast: the Sanskrit of dusk that speaks
in a glowing tongue of joy.
High overhead flow cigarette firelets
no one is smoking.
Sheets of blazing secrets aflame;
what the serenely fading sky tells
can't be remembered or even described.
So what if Pharaoh's armies pursue you,
when eternity is woven
through the days of the week like moss
in the chinks of a cabin?

ANTON BRUCKNER

For Renata Gorczynski

Dawn, and the scent of clover rises from low meadows.
Baroque churches press into the earth.
Peasant carts rumble through fog, geese quietly lament.
Practicing elocution like a timid Demosthenes,
the Danube flows over flat stones.
Mice run races through tunnels of hay.
In dark farmyards, lamps waver,
fearful shadows skim walls.
Sparrows try to sound human.
The manes of the horses are tangled, in the barn yellow straw.
Breath streaming, purple hands numb.
The world's too corporeal, obvious, dense,
its mutations have no design;
mirrors tire, reflecting
the same to and fro. Even an echo stammers.
At the door of a whitewashed cottage, a boy stands,
homely, with a too thick neck.
He is pious and good, though unappealing to girls.
Heavy boots, a bundle on his back.
Raindrops in a quizzical key drip from the roof.
The well pulley squeals, chairs speak in small voices.
The line dividing the spheres, where is it? Where are the sentries?
What do the elements lead and oxygen have to do with each other,
the torpid stone walls and the music that breathlessly
soars, freeing itself from the burden
of oboe, tuba, and horn, yet bound perpetually
to them so that the drums of hide
run with the spears of violas
and float in the rhythms of somnolent dances,
and in that breathtaking race, not, ever, a flight,
the shimmering Danube will vanish, and the cathedral of Linz

with its two domes, and even majestic Vienna, the Emperor's golden grain sown in its fertile gardens, will fall far behind, an insignificant dot on a map.

Anton Bruckner leaves home.

NIGHT

Because you're only dead,
I'm sure we'll meet again.
You'll still be nine,
as you were when I last
saw you in the mountains.
A late afternoon in August,
ripe, transparent,
the cherry tree's leaves unstirring,
the grasses mute.
Currants, already black, burst
on the tongue, their sweetness
holding the memory
of spring and summer, of storms,
and mornings, and the flight of a lark.
Running before us, laughing,
you could feel our tenderness
that followed you as lightly
as the breath of a sleeper.
You disappeared into the trees,
the shadows of firs. Evening approached,
and coolness, in the green shade of the firs.
We stood in the last rays of the sun,
we called calmly, "Where are you?"
We were so close to each other,
with only the whistle of sleepy birds
between us, and the vaults of the tangled branches.
Night slowly climbed
its corridors and tunnels.
Night passed through day.

ELEGY FOR THE LIVING

The joy of the moment turns suddenly
into a black hood with openings
only for eyes, mouth, tongue, grief. More grief.
The living see off their days
that flee
like negatives, exposed once
but never developed.

The living exist, so light-mindedly, so nonchalantly,
that the dead are abashed.
They smile sadly: Children,
we were like you, just the same.
Above us, robinias blossomed,
and in the robinias, nightingales sang.

BURGUNDY'S GRASSLANDS

Burgundy's grasslands scale the hills,
then lie still, inert as clothes
on a hanger. Despairing, we know nothing, nothing.
Minimalist memory, restricting itself
to what actually happened, is helpless
before Romanesque schemes that weren't built.
A surveyor-raven methodically measures a field.
Ash trees no one would accuse of being aesthetes
erect lush, leafy tents.
Larks race madly from one cloud
to another, like waiters on Sundays in crowded cafés.
We know nothing. Weeds sprout faster than our thoughts.

In a village church not far from Vézelay,
there's no one but a priest, no longer young,
who sings Mass,
so utterly alone that the tear which gathered
for three hundred years behind the eyelid of a cracked bell
is ready finally to fall.
Then stops. No, not yet,
not as long as the lonely keep singing.

ELECTRIC ELEGY

For Robert Hass

Farewell, German radio with your green eye
and your bulky box,
together almost composing
a body and soul. (Your lamps glowed
with a pink, salmony light, like Bergson's
deep self.)
          Through the thick fabric
of the speaker (my ear glued to you as
to the lattice of a confessional), Mussolini once whispered,
Hitler shouted, Stalin calmly explained,
Bierut hissed, Gomułka held endlessly forth.
But no one, radio, will accuse you of treason;
no, your only sin was obedience: absolute,
tender faithfulness to the megahertz;
whoever came was welcomed, whoever was sent
was received.
          Of course I know only
the songs of Schubert brought you the jade
of true joy. To Chopin's waltzes
your electric heart throbbed delicately
and firmly and the cloth over the speaker
pulsated like the breasts of amorous girls
in old novels.
          Not with the news, though,
especially not Radio Free Europe or the BBC.
Then your eye would grow nervous,
the green pupil widen and shrink
as though its atropine dose had been altered.
Mad seagulls lived inside you, and Macbeth.
At night, forlorn signals found shelter
in your rooms, sailors cried out for help,

the young comet cried, losing her head.
Your old age was announced by a cracked voice,
then rattles, coughing, and finally blindness
(your eye faded), and total silence.
Sleep peacefully, German radio,
dream Schumann and don't waken
when the next dictator-rooster crows.

SEPTEMBER AFTERNOON IN THE ABANDONED BARRACKS

The sun, the opulent sun of September,
the full sun of harvest and stubbled field,
stood still above me
and above the abandoned barracks.
Silence
bivouacked where once orders
were shouted;
silence, not
soldiers; in the infirmary
silence, not the groans
of the ill.
The overgrown grass in the yard
needs mowing.
Silence where blue-skulled
recruits sobbed.
In me, too, silence,
no longer despair.
A black rooster, a hot, black banner of blood,
runs down a path.
Autumn fades,
war dims.

MATCHES

Nothing's final, not even
deception. Matches sleep in a cloud
of brown dreams on their back.
True fire hasn't been born
yet, godparents
wait, trout swim
upstream. Back home, small world wars
flare, a table
frowns, a curtain's brow
obliquely touches the street. Evening
is sad as a Jew whose train
hasn't come, and the stationmaster
suspects. This makes more
sense, perhaps it's a prayer,
don't rush, though.
Sometimes diminishment swells
like dough for a Sunday bread.
If I'm only part
of this poem, why does it all stay silent?
Why should God give singing to thrushes,
and bolts of lightning
put gloves on their flames?

THE GOTHIC

For Ed Cohen

Who am I here in this cool cathedral and who
is speaking to me so obscurely?
Who am I, suddenly subject to a new atmospheric
pressure? Whose voices fill
this stone space? Voices of carpenters,
ashes of ash now? Voices
of vanished pilgrims
who still can't stay still?
Who am I, interred in this slim vault,
where is my name,
who's trying to snatch and hurl it away
like wind stealing a cap?

Small demons in bodies
borrowed from bestiaries peer down
like swimmers from diving boards
to the ocean of green earth
below them.
          The languid demons
of torture cells in provincial
cities, small
communists with stiff little hearts.
Oh, they too were created,
like leaves, lizards, and nettles:
they bud on the church,
leaned out, half wind, half
stone, the rain
flushing their throats
like political speeches—progress,
party, treason: their mutters flow

like rivers poured
through the funnel of the larynx.

Don't listen to this cascade of artifice,
go back to the nave, the heart
in its ribs of granite, the whirling,
pointed life of the Gothic arches
lazily combing time, enduring
in their forthright prayer
like theodicies in a meadow.
Go find the height again, and the dark,
where longing, pain, and joy live
and faith in the good God who does
and undoes, kindles
and extinguishes light and desire,
and who writes with his quill of years
long reminiscences
on the loveliest faces;
who tempts Abraham, casts up the domes
of Rome and the Auschwitz barracks, sings
lullabies to mute rivers and dims
in the lightning: go back, back
where concentration looms like a lake
in the mountains, where the metal
of illuminations and prayers cools.

Lost, circling in the cathedral
as suddenly vast as a Babylonian square,
evening now, dark, you hear alien voices,
whispers, calls: swallows
whistle, someone wails
with the voice of a suffering older than Cain's.
Far off, shutters close to stay closed
forever, and yellowish earth falls
on an oak board like a drum.

Someone is laughing aloud; you're alone,
no orator and no guide, trekking
a forest, huge ferns just out of sight,
herbs, flowers—white morning glories—
exhaling; sometimes the dead will find
a kind word, the ash leaves will glimmer;
owls flit softly through the vines
and the trees open, just this much, to utter
one sound.

        I feel
your presence in the bright gloom,
a sheet of torn paper, healing, healing
again, no trace, no scar. I hear
languages, voices, sighs,
the hopeful laments of those who loved
and those who preferred hatred, those who betrayed
and those betrayed, all of them
voyage in the labyrinth, above them
the fire soaring, the pure fire
of salutation and presence.
I feel you, I listen
to your silence.

PASSWORD

Look, your life, too, is becoming
the oil in a lamp on whose surface
the weak blue flame of homeland wanders.
That land, like depression, will steal
your youth and turn it into a password,
will take your rapture and give grief;
that land, that clock that won't run,
black band on a sleeve,
that land where souls are in storage
and bodies are no one's because death
is paid in advance and will come,
too early, at dawn, with its forehead of an ape,
too early, the clouds of morning, too early,
a prayer, kiss, the helpless children
fallen too early, and instead of orchids
the ashes of mountain September, cold fog,
the consoling lie, booze, not hell.

THE BLACKENED RIVER

The blackened river ran through the park.
Farther on, the numb gardens
were hemmed in by thick braids of hedges.
Where starlings sang now, a branch
of Auschwitz had been built:
under
the grass the dressings
from the Russian infirmary were interred,
so the meadow
is swollen and rich.
Gliders guiltlessly hovered in the sky,
in rain as benign as a tear of joy.

MOTHS

Moths watched us through
the window. Seated at the table,
we were skewered by their lambent gazes,
harder than their shattering wings.

You'll always be outside,
past the pane. And we'll be here within,
more and more in. Moths watched us
through the window, in August.

VACATION

The dark hair of summer. Beech leaves as tense
as the strings on a child's violin.
Rain, disoriented in the interminable drains
of a village church, blubbers.
Rembrandt, young, still unafraid,
watches from a postcard.
The sea lashes the rock so furiously
that someone mutters: war's coming.
Yesterday's sun still cools in the bricks.
Two cyclists in stiff capes
are crossing the bridge.
A green lightning of chickadees
glistens in the garden. The asphalt steams humbly
as though a barber had left his shaving bowl on it.
You sigh with relief: it's only
the weary pilgrims come home,
bearing the sugared bread of forgetfulness, exaltation,
silence.

WATCHING *SHOAH* IN A
HOTEL ROOM IN AMERICA

There are nights as soft as fur on a foal
but we prefer chess or card playing. Here,
some hotel guests sing "Happy Birthday"
as the one-eyed TV nonchalantly shuffles its images.
The trees of my childhood have crossed an ocean
to greet me coolly from the screen.
Polish peasants engage with a Jesuitical zest
in theological disputes: only the Jews are silent,
exhausted by their long dying.
The rivers of the voyages of my youth flow
cautiously over the distant, unfamiliar continent.
Hay wagons haul not hay, but hair,
their axles squeaking under the feathery weight.
We are innocent, the pines claim.
The SS officers are haggard and old,
doctors struggle to save them their hearts, lives, consciences.
It's late, the insinuations of drowsiness have me.
I'd sleep but my neighbors
choir "Happy Birthday" still louder:
louder than the dying Jews.
Huge trucks transport stars from the firmament,
gloomy trains go by in the rain.
I am innocent, Mozart repents;
only the aspen, as usual, trembles,
prepared to confess all its crimes.
The Czech Jews sing the national anthem: "Where is my home . . ."
There is no home, houses burn, the cold gas whistles within.
I grow more and more innocent, sleepy.
The TV reassures me: both of us
are beyond suspicion.

The birthday is noisier.
The shoes of Auschwitz, in pyramids
high as the sky, groan faintly:
Alas, we outlived mankind, now
let us sleep, sleep:
we have nowhere to go.

A fence. Chestnut trees. Bindweed. God.
A spiderweb, the hiding place
of first cause, and the thick grass:
between its blades shine the proofs of existence
like negatives drying.
The smell of braids and of wind
plaited in the mouth of the loved one.
Sour, the crushed stem
under the tongue.
Blackberries won't be
the apple of our discord.
Windflowers by the creek,
a ball gets away from the girl
and ripe, yellow hawthorns
sway softly.
Turn off the glaring sun,
listen to the tale of the seed of a poppy.
A fence. Chestnut trees. Bindweed. God.

AT MIDNIGHT

We'd talked long into the night
in the kitchen; the oil lamp glowed softly,
and objects, heartened by its calm,
came forth from the dark to offer
their names: chair, table, pitcher.

At midnight you said, Come out,
and in the dark there we saw the sky of August
explode with its stars.
Eternal, unconfined, night's pale sheen
trembled above us.

The world noiselessly burned,
white fire enveloped it all, villages,
churches, haystacks scented with clover
and mint. Trees burned, and spires,
wind, flame, water and air.

Why is night so silent if volcanoes
keep their eyes open and if the past
stays present, threatening, lurking
in its lair like junipers or the moon?
Your lips are cool, and the dawn will be, too,
a cloth on a feverish brow.

TO MYSELF, IN AN ALBUM

The grayish cloud flows fast,
the petals of peonies unfold,
nothing links you to this earth,
nothing binds you to this sky.

Distant gardens loom in the heat,
a cat yawns on a porch,
you walk a street of lindens,
but you don't know which town's.

You can't remember in which country
gleam airy starlings,
evening's step gently approaches,
rosebuds play hide-and-seek.

You're only an image, a dream,
you're made up wholly of yearning;
when you vanish, so will clouds,
you'll be a memory in sepia.

You'll haunt rural rivers,
and the shadows of trees,
but finally you'll subside, drowning
in the earth, in the earth, in the earth.

AUTUMN

Autumn is always too early.
The peonies are still blooming, bees
are still working out ideal states,
and the cold bayonets of autumn
suddenly glint in the fields and the wind
rages.

What is its origin? Why should it destroy
dreams, arbors, memories?
The alien enters the hushed woods,
anger advancing, insinuating plague;
woodsmoke, the raucous howls
of Tatars.

Autumn rips away leaves, names,
fruit, it covers the borders and paths,
extinguishes lamps and tapers; young
autumn, lips purpled, embraces
mortal creatures, stealing
their existence.

Sap flows, sacrificed blood,
wine, oil, wild rivers,
yellow rivers swollen with corpses,
the curse flowing on: mud, lava, avalanche,
gush.

Breathless autumn, racing, blue
knives glinting in her glance.
She scythes names like herbs with her keen
sickle, merciless in her blaze
and her breath. Anonymous letter, terror,
Red Army.

THE BELLS

For C. K. Williams

We'll take refuge in bells, in the swinging bells,
in the peal, the air, the heart of ringing.
We'll take refuge in bells and we'll float
over the earth in their heavy casings. Over the earth,
over fields, toward meadows, carried
by young ash trees, toward village churches
under the veil of haze in the morning and forests
stampeding like antelope herds; towards mills soundlessly turning
waterwheels by the stream. Over the earth, over meadows
and a single white daisy, over the bench on which love
carved its imperfect symbol, over a willow
obedient to the will of cool wind,
over the school where Latin words chat
in the evening; over the deep pond,
over the Tatras' green lake, over crying
and mourning, over binoculars shining
in sun, over calendars which filled themselves
with time and lie at the bottom of drawers
as peacefully as amphoras in oceans.
Over the border, over your attentive gaze,
over the pupil of somebody's eye, over a rusty cannon,
over the garden gate which no longer exists,
over clouds, over rain drinking dew,
over a snail unaware whose statue
it's climbing, over a gasping
express train, over a boy
knotting a tie before a school dance,
over the town park where a Swiss Army knife,
lost lifetimes ago, lies hidden still.
When the night comes, we'll take refuge
in bells, those airy carriages,
those bronze balloons.

THE CLOSE OF SUMMER

The commuter train speeds through detachments
of suburbs like a dagger hungry only for the heart.
The voice of some dictator or other
comes closer to me through the speakers
and a squirrel leaping from branch to branch
moves farther away.
The close of summer, cedar cones heavy,
a nun in a coarse brown habit
smiling like someone who's accepted it all.
Dragonflies skim the oily sheen of a pond,
rowboats slide then go down in the setting sun's crimson;
the heat, like a customs officer, palpates
each thing in its skin.
A mailman dozes on a bench and letters leap
from his bag like swallows; ice cream melts on the grass,
moles pile up mounds honoring swarthy heroes
nameless forever. Dark trees
stand above us, green fire between them.
September approaches; war, death.

APES

One day apes made their grab for power.
Gold seal-rings,
starched shirts,
aromatic Havanas,
feet squashed into patent leather.
Deeply involved in our other pursuits,
we didn't notice: someone read Aristotle,
someone else was wholly in love.
Rulers' speeches became somewhat more chaotic,
they even gibbered, but still, when
did we ever really listen? Music was better.
Wars: ever more savage; prisons:
stinking worse than before.
Apes, it seems, made their grab for power.

IN STRANGE CITIES

In strange cities, there's an unexpected joy,
the cool pleasure of a new regard.
The yellowing façades of tenements
the sun scales like an agile spider
aren't mine. The town hall,
harbor, jail and courthouse
weren't built for me either.
The sea runs through the city, its salty tide
submerging porches and basements.
In the market, pyramids of apples
rise for the eternity of one afternoon.
Even the suffering's not really mine:
the local madman mutters
in an alien language, the misery
of a lonely girl in a café
is like a piece of canvas in a dingy museum.
The huge flags of the trees, though,
flutter as in places we know,
and the same lead is sewn in the hems
of winding-sheets, dreams, and the imagination,
homeless, and mad.

SEVENTEEN

The adolescent Franz Schubert,
seventeen, composes music
to the wails of Faust's Gretchen, a girl his own age.
Meine Ruh' ist hin, mein Herz ist schwer.
Immediately that noted talent scout, Death,
fawning all over him, signs him up.
Sends invitations, one after another.
One. After. Another. Schubert asks
for indulgence, he doesn't want to arrive
empty-handed. But how ungracious to refuse.
Fourteen years later he gives
his first concert on the other side.
Why does charity kill, why does being strong blind?
Meine Ruh' ist hin, mein Herz ist schwer.

WITHOUT FORM

If there was just this,
a tree on which a star sleeps,
the empty cathedral at Chartres
and an impatient guide
and women waiting for their train
and music cold as longing?
If there was just this,
governments hiring ministers
and ministers hiring police
and a tiny angel
kissing their waxen lips in bed,
and dissidents protesting
and protesters marching
with smiling children
and music cold as longing
and the force never sleeping?
If there was just this,
poets' death masks and the skeletons
of giants in high mountains
and books on organisms' orgasm
and well-dressed blacks who don't
see me, and Keats crying
and those who're absent and traces
as light as the arsenic
in Napoleon's hair, and immobile masks
on petrified faces; the closed museums
of dreams and the force not wanting
to sleep and the Masonic symbols
Mozart hid even in his Requiem,
so cheating God: so much unexpressed,
and women, who have to live in our moment

without having asked to,
and countries, free once,
peeled now like apples,
and the weather, which changes, and I, myself, mature,
without form.

MOSES

Rivers rustling, martins preparing for flight.
Reeds like silent chaperons in ponds.
Mouths of so many cities, eyes of so many houses.
Glance of mankind, where are you?
Perpetual wind. Perpetual clouds, thirsty
for impermanence, drink time
as from cups stained with lipstick.
Farewell, warm bricks; shutters, farewell.

Day draws to its end, locomotives drowse
beneath plumes of flowering robinia,
snakes sway down narrow paths,
the small sun falls into a reed raft like Moses,
elated owls cry somber passwords,
a first star whistles in the sky,
the covetous fingers of nettles grow quickly.
Where are you, gaze of exaltation?
Everything's boredom without you.

THE LIGHT OF LAMPS

In memory of Constantin Jelenski

A dose of death occupied your body,
but it does everyone's:
I didn't realize
it would conquer so soon.
You laughed with the courage
of a fire-eater of eternity.
As a soldier in your youth, you'd defeated
the Third Reich reading books in a tank,
but you marched the boulevard Saint-Germain
like Montgomery,
against a sunset so huge
it wouldn't fit down the rows of buildings.
We knew nothing of each other,
being friends.
Now some streets are scars,
to be detoured.
Our one summer in the South was scorching; forests were afire.
In a Métro station in the suburbs once,
the two of us, foreigners,
disappeared into the earth,
in cold rain, the gleam of neon
dissolving in dampness like gouache.
In the kitchen of your flat once,
on the rue de La Vrillière,
we watched a white cat
drink from the tap.
There'll be no other "once."
You live in the shade now.
Moths should learn to navigate darkness,
since they so quickly find light.

WIND AT NIGHT

The wind rose at night,
the young, short-tempered wind,
a bubbling wine, Eastern prince.
It spoke indistinctly, in the accents
of languages living and dead.
Babylon's curses whirled within it,
the bells of Byzantium pealed.
Beneath its imperious blow, trees
obediently bent,
the shutters shook on our flimsy cottage.
We heard those voices with half
our attention, and, understanding little,
turned again to sleep, and to love.

WILD CHERRIES

Wild cherries sprout on slim
stems, pits wrapped
in pink flesh. Here, sparrows can spend hours
confessing to a stern vicar's ear,
loudly betraying non-venial sins
perpetrated at dawn.
Here, roses bloom half wild, too;
their petals hide missives
from the lost at sea and the unrequited,
to whom no one dedicates poems; at their cores
nestle quiet drops of dew;
bitter almonds. Sunday morning
a mother irons white shirts.
The State is perfect, the weather fine.
When you leave, the door immediately
weighs heavier than denunciation.
Thirst can't be quenched.
Behind the soccer field, wild cherries
sprout on slim stems, tart
by day, sweet when asleep.

ISLANDS AND TOWERS

Islands and towers I visited in the dreams
of my friends scattered all over the world.
They stood in the phosphorescence of memory, patient,
framed by towns at the limits of empires,
dried arbors, barbed hawthorns,
wooden steps bowed by the scuffle of feet,
in schoolrooms, hospitals like scars, concrete apartments.

Ironically smiling, you stood erect,
as though posing for a provincial photographer,
sure that we always know more than the film
can convey, more than a lens scrawls in its polar frenzy,
more than what's left of us
in an image, intention, thought, deed.

Snatched out of the Greenwich meridian, or Krakow's cathedral
where the hours are announced by a bugle, on leave from Hegel's
       system,
you looked at me with the open gaze of portraits
in the Louvre: in the street, streams
of spring rain flowed, lightning flashed
on the panes, stores of poetry melted.

That each failure is different: what consolation.
That each task has its own name,
each drama unfolds in a different place,
with a different ending; silence, tears, fright,
joy, vision, success, a hymn; it ends in a church,
empty train, jail, lecture hall, mud.

A HISTORY OF SOLITUDE

Birdsong diminishes.
The moon sits for a photo.
The wet cheeks of streets gleam.
Wind brings the scent of ripe fields.
High overhead, a small plane cavorts like a dolphin.

FROM THE LIVES OF THINGS

The perfect skin of things is stretched across them
as snugly as a circus tent.
Evening nears.
Welcome, darkness.
Farewell, daylight.
We're like eyelids, assert things,
we touch eyes, hair, darkness,
light, India, Europe.

Suddenly I find myself asking: "Things,
do you know suffering?
Were you ever hungry, down and out?
Have you cried? Do you know fear,
shame? Have you learned jealousy, envy,
small sins, not of commission,
but not cured by absolution either?
Have you loved, and died,
at night, wind opening the windows, absorbing
the cool heart? Have you tasted
age, time, bereavement?"
Silence.
On the wall, the needle of a barometer dances.

CRUEL

For Joseph Czapski

In the Parc de Saint-Cloud, birds sang.
Alone in that vast, narcissistic forest
that looks out on Paris,
I pondered your words:
The world is cruel; rapacious,
carnivorous, cruel.

I circled the Parc de Saint-Cloud, east to west,
west to east,
I strolled through the leafless
chestnuts, bowed to the dark, bowing cedars,
heard pinecones cracked
by sparrows and wrens.
No beast of prey in the park,
other than time, just then changing
from winter to spring, stripped,
an actor flinging his costume away,
in the cold wings backstage.

Cruel? I thought. Here is the killer,
abetted by police and by priests—
even you've indulged it,
the protagonist
of your paintings. But is there a choice?
A world milder and softer?
Trees more exquisite, cedars
with still darker needles, more sumptuous
feasts, moments of meditation
thrusting to the core of knowledge?
Is there a kinder time, gentler, eager

to give back those we've lost, to restore us
to ourselves, pure, young?

A rose sky; tight, narrow ribbons of cloud.

The brown walls of prisons, hospitals, courts,
wailing corridors with no end,
moments of contemplation riven, imperiled
by terror, anxiety, lies.

I circled the Parc de Saint-Cloud, faster, faster,
winter over, spring not yet.
In the park, barren, bereft of its king,
I kept saying it, "Cruel," my only witnesses
lizards and birds.
Then, through a dense mist the white sun boiled:
I was impaled by sharp barbs of bliss.

SIMONE WEIL WATCHES THE RHÔNE VALLEY

I found her in front of the house, sitting on a stump,
sunk in contemplation of the Rhône Valley . . .
—Gustave Thibon

Suddenly she doesn't comprehend,
but only watches:
the Valley of the Rhône opens in the earth,
old villages appear above it,
broad scrawls of vineyards, thirsty wells.
The plane trees slowly reawaken,
roosters resume their stubborn march,
hawks mount the sky again,
and now she almost sees the light breath of larks,
mounds shouldered up by black moles,
farm roofs, walnut trees,
church towers curled like tobacco,
dark fields of ripe grain, scythes glittering,
baskets of grapes.
In the shade of the juniper death hovers,
war is near.
The broad Rhône's mercury oozes down the valley
with its barges and boats;
a moment of forgiveness,
an instant's bliss,
the olive tree of nothingness.

FRUIT

For Czeslaw Milosz

How unattainable life is, it only reveals
its features in memory,
in nonexistence. How unattainable
afternoons, ripe, tumultuous, leaves
bursting with sap; swollen fruit, the rustling
silks of women who pass on the other
side of the street, and the shouts of boys
leaving school. Unattainable. The simplest
apple inscrutable, round.
The crowns of trees shake in warm
currents of air. Unattainably distant mountains.
Intangible rainbows. Huge cliffs of clouds
flowing slowly through the sky. The sumptuous,
unattainable afternoon. My life,
swirling, unattainable, free.

CANVAS

I stood in silence before a dark picture,
before a canvas that might have been
coat, shirt, flag,
but had turned instead into the world.

I stood in silence before the dark canvas,
charged with delight and revolt and I thought
of the arts of painting and living,
of so many blank, bitter days,

of moments of helplessness
and my chilly imagination
that's the tongue of a bell,
alive only when swaying,

striking what it loves,
loving what it strikes,
and it came to me that this canvas
could have become a winding-sheet, too.

FROM

MYSTICISM FOR
BEGINNERS

(1997)

TRANSLATED BY CLARE CAVANAGH

A QUICK POEM

I was listening to Gregorian chants
in a speeding car
on a highway in France.
The trees rushed past. Monks' voices
sang praises to an unseen God
(at dawn, in a chapel trembling with cold).
Domine, exaudi orationem meam,
male voices pleaded calmly
as if salvation were just growing in the garden.
Where was I going? Where was the sun hiding?
My life lay tattered
on both sides of the road, brittle as a paper map.
With the sweet monks
I made my way toward the clouds, deep blue,
heavy, dense,
toward the future, the abyss,
gulping hard tears of hail.
Far from dawn. Far from home.
In place of walls—sheet metal.
Instead of a vigil—a flight.
Travel instead of remembrance.
A quick poem instead of a hymn.
A small, tired star raced
up ahead
and the highway's asphalt shone,
showing where the earth was,
where the horizon's razor lay in wait,
and the black spider of evening
and night, widow of so many dreams.

TRANSFORMATION

I haven't written a single poem
in months.
I've lived humbly, reading the paper,
pondering the riddle of power
and the reasons for obedience.
I've watched sunsets
(crimson, anxious),
I've heard the birds grow quiet
and night's muteness.
I've seen sunflowers dangling
their heads at dusk, as if a careless hangman
had gone strolling through the gardens.
September's sweet dust gathered
on the windowsill and lizards
hid in the bends of walls.
I've taken long walks,
craving one thing only:
lightning,
transformation,
you.

SEPTEMBER

For Petr Král

I was in Prague looking for Vladimir Holan's house,
the prison-house where he spent fifteen years.
(I thought I'd find it easily, roosters
would guide me and an old priest
in a neatly mended cassock would say:
here lived the poet, and suffering slept here
like a stray cat, hiding once a week
in a fur coat's sleeve.)
                        The light already felt like fall,
the sun was a bit offended. September kissed the hills
and treetops like someone leaving
on a long trip who realizes only at the station
that he's lost his keys.
Inside the labyrinth tourists moved warily,
consulting the black void of their cameras.
The elms' flames floated over parks
like Saint Elmo's fire. Bonfires in gardens
and gray smoke above the earth, the wells.
But chestnut leaves, light and dry,
like a certain kind of unconcerned old age,
kept sailing higher.
What are baroque churches? Deluxe
health clubs for athletic saints.
They didn't want to help me. (Whoever seeks another's home,
one handsome, learnèd angel whispered,
will never find his own.) No one would help me.
Children shrieked happily
for no reason (full of cruelty just in case).
The wind was full of air, the air full of oxygen,
the oxygen held memories of a trip beyond the sea.
Was I right, were the palaces' walls, yellowed

as from nicotine, absorbed in border disputes?
I couldn't find Holan's house.
Life triumphed, as always, but the dead poet
dwelled in oblivion, in the sparks shooting
from beneath the welder's palm, in my growing exhaustion.
Nowhere, nowhere, nowhere at all.
He comes here, but only at night,
someone finally told me who wasn't there.

MYSTICISM FOR BEGINNERS

The day was mild, the light was generous.
The German on the café terrace
held a small book on his lap.
I caught sight of the title:
Mysticism for Beginners.
Suddenly I understood that the swallows
patrolling the streets of Montepulciano
with their shrill whistles,
and the hushed talk of timid travelers
from Eastern, so-called Central Europe,
and the white herons standing—yesterday? the day before?—
like nuns in fields of rice,
and the dusk, slow and systematic,
erasing the outlines of medieval houses,
and olive trees on little hills,
abandoned to the wind and heat,
and the head of the *Unknown Princess*
that I saw and admired in the Louvre,
and stained-glass windows like butterfly wings
sprinkled with pollen,
and the little nightingale practicing
its speech beside the highway,
and any journey, any kind of trip,
are only mysticism for beginners,
the elementary course, prelude
to a test that's been
postponed.

THE THREE KINGS

We'll arrive too late . . .

—André Frénaud, "The Three Kings"

If it hadn't been for the desert and laughter and music—
we'd have made it, if our yearning
hadn't mingled with the highways' dust.
We saw poor countries, made still poorer
by their ancient hatred;
a train full of soldiers and refugees
stood waiting at a burning station.
We were heaped with great honors
so we thought—perhaps one of us
really is a king?
Spring meadows detained us, cowslips,
the glances of country maidens
hungry for a stranger's love.
We made offerings to the gods, but we don't know
if they recognized our faces
through the flame's honey-gold veil.
Once we fell asleep and slept for many months,
but dreams raged in us, heavy, treacherous,
like surf beneath a full moon.
Fear awakened us and again we moved on,
cursing fate and filthy inns.
For four years a cold wind blew,
but the star was yellow, sewn carelessly to a coat
like a school insignia.
The taxi smelled of anise and the twentieth century,
the driver had a Russian accent.
Our ship sank, the plane shook suddenly.
We quarreled violently and each of us
set out in search of a different hope.
I barely remember what we were looking for
and I'm not sure if a December night

will open up someday
like a camera's eye.
Perhaps I'd be happy, live content,
if it weren't for the light that explodes
above the city walls each day
at dawn, blinding my desire.

THE GREENHOUSE

In a small black town, your town,
where even trains linger unwilling,
anxious to be on their way,
in a park, defying soot and shadows,
a gray building stands lined with mother-of-pearl.

Forget the snow, the frost's repeated blows;
inside you're greeted by a damp anthology of breezes
and the enigmatic whispers of vast leaves
coiled like lazy snakes. Even an Egyptologist
couldn't make them out.

Forget the sadness of dark stadiums and streets,
the weight of thwarted Sundays.
Accept the warm breath wafting from the plants.
The gentle scent of faded lightning
engulfs you, beckoning you on.

Perhaps you see the rusty sails of ships at port,
islands snared in rosy mist, crumbling temples' towers;
you glimpse what you've lost, what never was,
and people with lives
like your own.

Suddenly you see the world lit differently,
other people's doors swing open for a moment,
you read their hidden thoughts, their holidays don't hurt,
their happiness is less opaque, their faces
almost beautiful.

Lose yourself, go blind from ecstasy,
forgetting everything, and then perhaps
a deeper memory, a deeper recognition will return,
and you'll hear yourself saying: I don't know how—
the palm trees opened up my greedy heart.

DUTCH PAINTERS

Pewter bowls heavy and swelling with metal.
Plump windows bulging from the light.
The palpability of leaden clouds.
Gowns like quilts. Moist oysters.
These things are immortal, but don't serve us.
The clogs walk by themselves.
The floor tiles are never bored,
and sometimes play chess with the moon.
An ugly girl studies a letter
written in invisible ink.
Is it about love or money?
The tablecloths smell of starch and morals.
The surface and depths don't connect.
Mystery? There's no mystery here, just blue sky,
restless and hospitable like a seagull's cry.
A woman neatly peeling a red apple.
Children dream of old age.
Someone reads a book (a book is read),
someone sleeps, becoming a warm object
that breathes like an accordion.
They liked dwelling. They dwelt everywhere,
in a wooden chair back,
in a milky streamlet narrow as the Bering Strait.
Doors were wide open, the wind was friendly.
Brooms rested after work well done.
Homes bared all. The painting of a land
without secret police.
Only on the young Rembrandt's face
an early shadow fell. Why?
Tell us, Dutch painters, what will happen

when the apple is peeled, when the silk dims,
when all the colors grow cold.
Tell us what darkness is.

POSTCARDS

The asters burn with the dim glow
of velvet ribbons.
Then the chrysanthemums,
a faded northern shade of yellow.

It was All Saints' Day
but we had nowhere to go.
Our dead don't dwell in this country,
they pitch their tents in other dead men's memories,
in the fruits of hawthorn and lead.

It had been raining for a week, raindrops
marched into the earth
like Chinese warriors with rigid faces.
Mountain streams lay on their backs
greedily lapping up water and October,
and the clay shaped
ever more perfect forms.

We had nowhere to go
although the day was empty
like a sleeve buoyed by the wind.
Cemeteries swarmed with elegant,
unseen guests,
like a ballroom at dawn
when dreams pale.

Our dead don't live in this country—
they've been traveling for years.
The address they give on yellowed postcards
can't be read, and the nations engraved
on the stamps have long since ceased to exist.

SHELL

At night the monks sang softly
and a gusting wind lifted
spruce branches like wings.
I've never visited the ancient cities,
I've never been to Thebes
or Delphi, and I don't know
what the oracles once told travelers.
Snow filled the streets and canyons,
and crows in dark robes silently
trailed the fox's footprints.
I believed in elusive signs,
in shadowed ruins, water snakes,
mountain springs, prophetic birds.
Linden trees bloomed like brides
but their fruit was small and bitter.
Wisdom can't be found
in music or fine paintings,
in great deeds, courage,
even love,
but only in all these things,
in earth and air, in pain and silence.
A poem may hold the thunder's echo,
like a shell touched by Orpheus
as he fled. Time takes life away
and gives us memory, gold with flame,
black with embers.

REFUGEES

Bent under burdens which sometimes
can be seen and sometimes can't,
they trudge through mud or desert sands,
hunched, hungry,

silent men in heavy jackets,
dressed for all four seasons,
old women with crumpled faces,
clutching something—a child, the family
lamp, the last loaf of bread?

It could be Bosnia today,
Poland in September '39, France
eight months later, Germany in '45,
Somalia, Afghanistan, Egypt.

There's always a wagon or at least a wheelbarrow
full of treasures (a quilt, a silver cup,
the fading scent of home),
a car out of gas marooned in a ditch,
a horse (soon left behind), snow, a lot of snow,
too much snow, too much sun, too much rain,

and always that special slouch
as if leaning toward another, better planet,
with less ambitious generals,
less snow, less wind, fewer cannons,
less History (alas, there's no
such planet, just that slouch).

Shuffling their feet,
they move slowly, very slowly
toward the country of nowhere,
and the city of no one
on the river of never.

LETTER FROM A READER

Too much about death,
too many shadows.
Write about life,
an average day,
the yearning for order.

Take the school bell
as your model
of moderation,
even scholarship.

Too much death,
too much
dark radiance.

Take a look,
crowds packed
in cramped stadiums
sing hymns of hatred.

Too much music,
too little harmony, peace,
reason.

Write about those moments
when friendship's footbridges
seem more enduring
than despair.

Write about love,
long evenings,

the dawn,
the trees,
about the endless patience
of the light.

I WASN'T IN THIS POEM

I wasn't in this poem,
only gleaming pure pools,
a lizard's tiny eye, the wind
and the sounds of a harmonica
pressed to not my lips.

FOR M.

I lay beneath the stars of another sky
in the black grass at midnight.
Midnight breathed, slow and lazy,
and I thought about you, about us,
about sharp and shining moments
plucked from my imagination like a thorn
drawn from an athlete's narrow foot.
That day the sea grew dark and
grim, the storm's orchids rushed
over crumpled sheets of water.
It could also have been childhood,
the land of easy ecstasy and endless longing,
red poppies in the lips of noon
and church towers alert as hummingbirds.
Soldiers walked along the street, but the war
was already over and rifles bloomed.
Some days the hush was so devout
we were afraid to move. A fox dashed across a field.
We tried the taste of leaves, the taste of light
that dazzles the innocent.
But the air had a bitter taste: carnations,
cinnamon, dust, and acorns,
winter, the first week of fall.
The bitter taste of unshed blood.
We stood a long time on the viaduct over the tracks
and a train must have passed under us;
only the dry sun was reflected
in its countless windows.
That's laughter, you said, that's iron,

salt, sand, glass.
                    And the future,
the fabric of your dress, life, which we shared
like a meal while traveling.

THAT'S SICILY

At night we sailed past shadowed,
enigmatic shores. Far off, the huge leaves
of hills swayed like a giant's dreams.
Waves slapped the boat's wood,
a warm wind kissed the sails,
stars rushed, helter-skelter,
to tell the history of the world.
That's Sicily, someone whispered,
three-cornered island, owl's breath,
handkerchief of the dead.

YOU ARE MY SILENT BRETHREN

You are my silent brethren,
the dead.
I won't forget you.

In old letters I find traces of your writing,
creeping to the page's top
like a snail on the wall of a psychiatric ward.

Your addresses and phone numbers pitch camp
in my notebooks, waiting, dozing.

I was in Paris yesterday, I saw hundreds of tourists,
tired and cold. I thought, they look
like you, they can't get settled, they circle restlessly.

You'd think it would be easy, living.
All you need is a fistful of earth, a boat, a nest, a jail,
a little breath, some drops of blood, and longing.

You are my masters,
the dead.
Don't forget me.

OUT WALKING

Sometimes out walking, on a country road
or in a quiet green forest,
you hear scraps of voices, perhaps they're calling you,
you don't want to believe them, you walk faster,
but they catch up quickly,
like tame animals.

You don't want to believe them, then later
on a busy city street
you're sorry you didn't listen
and you try to summon up
the syllables, the sounds, and the intervals between them.

But it's too late now
and you'll never know
who was singing, which song,
and where it was drawing you.

VERMEER'S LITTLE GIRL

Vermeer's little girl, now famous,
watches me. A pearl watches me.
The lips of Vermeer's little girl
are red, moist, and shining.

Oh Vermeer's little girl, oh pearl,
blue turban: you are all light
and I am made of shadow.
Light looks down on shadow
with forbearance, perhaps pity.

TIERRA DEL FUEGO

You who see our homes at night
and the frail walls of our conscience,
you who hear our conversations
droning on like sewing machines
—save me, tear me from sleep,
from amnesia.

Why is childhood—oh, tinfoil treasures,
oh, the rustling of lead, lovely and foreboding—
our only origin, our only longing?
Why is manhood, which takes the place of ripeness,
an endless highway,
Sahara yellow?

After all, you know there are days
when even thirst runs dry
and prayer's lips harden.

Sometimes the sun's coin dims
and life shrinks so small
that you could tuck it
in the blue gloves of the Gypsy
who predicts the future
for seven generations back

and then in some other little town
in the south a charlatan
decides to destroy you,
me, and himself.

You who see the whites of our eyes,
you who hide like a bullfinch
in the rowans,
like a falcon
in the clouds' warm stockings

—open the boxes full of song,
open the blood that pulses in aortas
of animals and stones,
light lanterns in black gardens.

Nameless, unseen, silent,
save me from anesthesia,
take me to Tierra del Fuego,
take me where the rivers
flow straight up, horizontal rivers
flowing up and down.

ALBI

The traveler greets his new setting,
hoping to find happiness there,
perhaps even his memory.

Albi opens before me—
an acacia leaf, soft and friendly

—but the basilica can't be vanquished,
its slick walls and dagger windows
deflect my emotions.

A west wind blows, from Spain,
bearing a drop of sorrow and an atom of ocean.
Plane trees greet each other
like courtiers in green gowns
dusty from a long carriage ride.

I still don't know what the world is,
a tall wave drowning the senses,
courage and peace and the still flames of lanterns
tonight as we bid the dead farewell;

fatigue and fertile dreams
pass through us like relentless pilgrims.

The patient basilica stands still.
Clouds swim, sleepy, lazy,
like a lowland river.
The fire-archer poises over me, fixed and shifting.

You're no longer here,
but I'm alive, alive and looking,
and the ball of my breath
rolls through narrow country roads.

SELF-PORTRAIT

Between the computer, a pencil, and a typewriter
half my day passes. One day it will be half a century.
I live in strange cities and sometimes talk
with strangers about matters strange to me.
I listen to music a lot: Bach, Mahler, Chopin, Shostakovich.
I see three elements in music: weakness, power, and pain.
The fourth has no name.
I read poets, living and dead, who teach me
tenacity, faith, and pride. I try to understand
the great philosophers—but usually catch just
scraps of their precious thoughts.
I like to take long walks on Paris streets
and watch my fellow creatures, quickened by envy,
anger, desire; to trace a silver coin
passing from hand to hand as it slowly
loses its round shape (the emperor's profile is erased).
Beside me trees expressing nothing
but a green, indifferent perfection.
Black birds pace the fields,
waiting patiently like Spanish widows.
I'm no longer young, but someone else is always older.
I like deep sleep, when I cease to exist,
and fast bike rides on country roads when poplars and houses
dissolve like cumuli on sunny days.
Sometimes in museums the paintings speak to me
and irony suddenly vanishes.
I love gazing at my wife's face.
Every Sunday I call my father.
Every other week I meet with friends,
thus proving my fidelity.
My country freed itself from one evil. I wish

another liberation would follow.
Could I help in this? I don't know.
I'm truly not a child of the ocean,
as Antonio Machado wrote about himself,
but a child of air, mint, and cello
and not all the ways of the high world
cross paths with the life that—so far—
belongs to me.

DECEMBER WIND

The December wind kills hope,
but don't let it take
the blue mist from the ocean
and the summer morning's mildness.

Who believes that invisible,
light islands still exist
and stains of sunshine
on a parquet floor?

Sleep wanders in rags
begging for alms
while memory, like Mary Stuart,
withers in a prison cell.

TRAVELER

A certain traveler, who believed in nothing,
found himself one summer in a foreign city.
Lindens were blossoming, and foreignness bloomed devoutly.

An unknown crowd walked down the fragrant boulevard,
slowly, full of fear, perhaps because
the setting sun weighed more than the horizon

and the asphalt's scarlet might not
just be shadows and the guillotine
might not grace museums alone

and church bells chiming in chorus
might mean more than they usually mean.
Perhaps that's why the traveler kept

putting his hand to his chest, checking warily
to make sure he still had his return ticket
to the ordinary places where we live.

THE HOUSE

Do you still remember what the house was like?
The house—a pocket in a snowstorm's overcoat,
houses, low and bulging like Egyptian vowels.
Sheltered by green tongues of trees—
the most faithful was the linden, it shed
dry tears each fall.
Outmoded dresses dangled in the attic
like hanged men. Old letters flamed.
The old piano dozing in the parlor,
a hippo with black and yellow teeth.
On the wall a cross from a failed uprising
hung crookedly, and a photo
of a sad girl—a failed life.
The air smelled like vermouth,
bitter and sweet at once.
Houses, houses, where are you,
under what ocean, in what memory,
beneath the roof of what existence?
While the wind was opening windows, a deep blue
past sneaked into the rooms
and stifled the muslin curtains' breathing.
The fire was death's intended
and brought her bouquets of pale sparks.

MOMENT

In the Romanesque church round stones
that ground down so many prayers and generations
kept humble silence and shadows slept in the apse
like bats in winter furs.

We went out. The pale sun shone,
tinny music tinkled softly
from a car, two jays
studied us, humans,
threads of longing dangled in the air.

The present moment is shameless,
taking its foolish liberties
beside the wall
of this tired old shrine,

awaiting the millions of years to come,
future wars, geological eras,
cease-fires, treaties, changes in climate—
this moment—what is it—just

a mosquito, a fly, a speck, a scrap of breath,
and yet it's taken over everywhere,
entering the timid grass,
inhabiting stems and genes,
the pupils of our eyes.

This moment, mortal as you or I,
was full of boundless, senseless,
silly joy, as if it knew
something we didn't.

BLACKBIRD

A blackbird sat on the TV antenna
and sang a gentle, jazzy tune.
Whom have you lost, I asked, what do you mourn?
I'm taking leave of those who've gone, the blackbird said,
I'm parting with the day (its eyes and lashes),
I mourn a girl who lived in Thrace,
you wouldn't know her.
I'm sorry for the willow, killed by frost.
I weep, since all things pass and alter
and return, but always in a different form.
My narrow throat can barely hold
the grief, despair, delight, and pride
occasioned by such sweeping transformations.
A funeral cortege passes up ahead,
the same each evening, there, on the horizon's thread.
Everyone's there, I see them all and bid farewell.
I see the swords, hats, kerchiefs, and bare feet,
guns, blood, and ink. They walk slowly
and vanish in the river mist, on the right bank.
I say goodbye to them and you and the light,
and then I greet the night, since I serve her—
and black silks, black powers.

ELEGY

It was a gray landscape, houses small
as Tartar ponies, concrete high-rises,
massive, stillborn; uniforms everywhere, rain,
drowsy rivers not knowing where to flow,
dust, Soviet gods with swollen eyelids,
sour smell of gas, sweet smell of tedium,
grimy trains, the red-eyed dawn.

It was a little landscape, endless winters,
in which there dwelled, as if in ancient lindens,
sparrows and knives and friendship and leaves of treason;
the arcs of village streets; pinched meadows; on a park bench
someone idly played the accordion
and for a moment you could breathe air
lighter than fatigue.

It was a waiting room with brown walls,
a courtroom, a clinic; a room
where tables slumped under files
and ashtrays choked on ashes.
It was silence or loudspeakers shrieking.
A waiting room where you waited
a lifetime to be born.

Our short-lived loves lasting so long,
our mighty laughter, ironies and triumphs
perhaps still fading in a police station
on the map's margin, on the edge of imagination.
The voices, the hair of the dead.
The chronometers of our desire,
a time full of emptiness.

It was a black landscape, only the mountains were blue
and a rainbow sloped. There were no promises, no hopes,
but we lived there, and not as strangers.
It was the life we'd been given.
It was patience, glacier-pale.
It was fear full of guilt. Courage
full of anxiety. Anxiety filled with power.

CELLO

Those who don't like it say it's
just a mutant violin
that's been kicked out of the chorus.
Not so.
The cello has many secrets,
but it never sobs,
just sings in its low voice.
Not everything turns into song
though. Sometimes you catch
a murmur or a whisper:
I'm lonely,
I can't sleep.

DEGAS: *THE MILLINER'S SHOP*

The hats are innocent, bathed
in a soft light blurring their forms.
The girl is hard at work.
But where are the brooks? The groves?
Where's the sensuous laughter of nymphs?
The world is hungry, and one day
it will invade this peaceful room.
For the time being it's appeased by ambassadors
announcing: I'm ocher.
And I'm sienna. I'm the color of terror,
like ash. Ships drown in me.
I'm the color blue, I'm cold,
I can be ruthless.
And I'm the color of death,
I'm endlessly patient.
I'm purple (you can barely see me),
triumphs and parades are mine.
I'm green, I'm tender,
I live in wells and birch leaves.
The girl, with her deft fingers,
doesn't hear the voices, since she's mortal.
She thinks about next Sunday,
and her date with the butcher's son
who has thick lips
and big hands
stained with blood.

PLANETARIUM

Let's say it was September.
An artificial sky revolved above us.
Us, the school class. Me, my eyes,
my easy life, my sixteen years.
On the ceiling stars like dancers
made appearances, comets hurried
on their errands to the far ends of the earth.
The small explosions on the screen—
the loudspeaker explained—are in fact
terrifyingly vast, but essential
and predictable.
        Let's suppose that for a second
the lights dimmed and darkness fell,
a black wind blew.
It seemed to be raining, hailing,
a thunderstorm approached, someone yelled
for help, begged the real
stars to return.
        Let's say they came back
and their light was blinding.

SHE WROTE IN DARKNESS

To Ryszard Krynicki
While living in Stockholm Nelly Sachs
worked at night by a dim lamp,
so as not to waken her sick mother.

She wrote in darkness.
Despair dictated words
heavy as a comet's tail.

She wrote in darkness,
in silence broken only
by the wall clock's sighs.

Even the letters grew drowsy,
their heads drooping on the page.

Darkness wrote,
having taken this middle-aged woman
for its fountain pen.

Night took pity on her,
morning's gray prison
rose over the city,
rosy-fingered dawn.

While she dozed off
the blackbirds woke
and there was no break
in the sorrow and song.

AIRPORT IN AMSTERDAM

In memory of my mother

December rose, pinched desire
in the dark and empty garden,
rust on the trees and thick smoke
as if someone's loneliness were burning.

Out walking yesterday I thought again
about the airport in Amsterdam—
the corridors without apartments,
waiting rooms filled with other people's dreams
stained with misfortune.

Airplanes struck the cement
almost angrily, hawks
without prey, hungry.

Maybe your funeral should have been held
here—hubbub, bustling crowds,
a good place not to be.

One has to look after the dead
beneath the airport's great tent.
We were nomads again;
you wandered westward in your summer dress,
amazed by war and time,
the moldering ruins, the mirror
reflecting a little, tired life.

In the darkness final things shone:
the horizon, a knife, and every rising sun.
I saw you off at the airport, hectic
valley where tears are for sale.

December rose, sweet orange:
without you there can be
no Christmases.

Mint leaves soothe a migraine . . .
In restaurants you always
studied the menu longest . . .
In our ascetic family
you were the mistress of expression,
but you died so quietly . . .

The old priest will garble your name.
The train will halt in the forest.
At dawn snow will fall
on the airport in Amsterdam.

Where are you?
There where memory lies buried.
There where memory grows.
There where the orange, rose, and snow lie buried.
There where ashes grow.

NIGHT

Dances beautifully
and has great desires.
Seeks the road.
Weeps in the woods.
Is killed by dawn, fever,
and the rooster.

LONG AFTERNOONS

Those were the long afternoons when poetry left me.
The river flowed patiently, nudging lazy boats to sea.
Long afternoons, the coast of ivory.
Shadows lounged in the streets, haughty manikins in shopfronts
stared at me with bold and hostile eyes.

Professors left their schools with vacant faces,
as if the *Iliad* had finally done them in.
Evening papers brought disturbing news,
but nothing happened, no one hurried.
There was no one in the windows, you weren't there;
even nuns seemed ashamed of their lives.

Those were the long afternoons when poetry vanished
and I was left with the city's opaque demon,
like a poor traveler stranded outside the Gare du Nord
with his bulging suitcase wrapped in twine
and September's black rain falling.

Oh, tell me how to cure myself of irony, the gaze
that sees but doesn't penetrate; tell me how to cure myself
of silence.

TO MY OLDER BROTHER

How calmly we walk
through the days and months,
how softly we sing
our black lullaby,
how easily wolves seize
our brothers,
how gently
death breathes,
how swiftly
ships swim
in our arteries.

THE CITY WHERE I WANT TO LIVE

The city is quiet at dusk,
when pale stars waken from their swoon,
and resounds at noon with the voices
of ambitious philosophers and merchants
bearing velvet from the East.
The flames of conversation burn there,
but not pyres.
Old churches, the mossy stones
of ancient prayer, are both its ballast
and its rocket ship.
It is a just city
where foreigners aren't punished,
a city quick to remember
and slow to forget,
tolerating poets, forgiving prophets
for their hopeless lack of humor.
The city was based
on Chopin's preludes,
taking from them only joy and sorrow.
Small hills circle it
in a wide collar; ash trees
grow there, and the slim poplar,
chief justice in the state of trees.
The swift river flowing through the city's heart
murmurs cryptic greetings
day and night
from the springs, the mountains, and the sky.

PERSEPHONE

Persephone goes underground again
in a summer dress, with a Jewish
child's big eyes.

Kites fly, and yellow leaves, autumn dust,
a white plane, black crow wings.
Someone runs down the path clutching an overdue letter.

She'll be cold underground in cork
sandals and her hair won't shield
her from the blind wind, from oblivion—

she disappears into the chestnut trees
and only the ribbon on her braid
shines with resignation's rosy glow.

Persephone goes underground again
and again the same thread of indifference
binds my tiny bird-heart.

THE ROOM I WORK IN

To Derek Walcott

The room I work in is as foursquare
as half a pair of dice.
It holds a wooden table
with a stubborn peasant's profile,
a sluggish armchair, and a teapot's
pouting Hapsburg lip.
From the window I see a few skinny trees,
wispy clouds, and toddlers,
always happy and loud.
Sometimes a windshield glints in the distance
or, higher up, an airplane's silver husk.
Clearly others aren't wasting time
while I work, seeking adventures
on earth or in the air.
The room I work in is a camera obscura.
And what is my work—
waiting motionless,
flipping pages, patient meditation,
passivities not pleasing
to that judge with the greedy gaze.
I write as slowly as if I'll live two hundred years.
I seek images that don't exist,
and if they do they're crumpled and concealed
like summer clothes in winter,
when frost stings the mouth.
I dream of perfect concentration; if I found it
I'd surely stop breathing.
Maybe it's good I get so little done.
But after all, I hear the first snow hissing,

the frail melody of daylight,
and the city's gloomy rumble.
I drink from a small spring,
my thirst exceeds the ocean.

THREE ANGELS

Suddenly three angels appeared
right here by the bakery on St. George Street.
Not another census bureau survey,
one tired man sighed.
No, the first angel said patiently,
we just wanted to see
what your lives have become,
the flavor of your days and why
your nights are marked by restlessness and fear.

That's right, fear, a lovely, dreamy-eyed
woman replied; but I know why.
The labors of the human mind have faltered.
They seek help and support
they can't find. Sir, just take a look
—she called the angel "Sir"!—
at Wittgenstein. Our sages
and leaders are melancholy madmen
and know even less than us
ordinary people (but she wasn't
ordinary).

Then too, said one boy
who was learning to play the violin, evenings
are just an empty carton,
a casket minus mysteries,
while at dawn the cosmos seems as
parched and foreign as a TV screen.
And besides, those who love music for itself
are few and far between.

Others spoke up and their laments
surged into a swelling sonata of wrath.
If you gentlemen want to know the truth,
one tall student yelled—he'd
just lost his mother—we've had enough
of death and cruelty, persecution, disease,
and long spells of boredom still
as a serpent's eye. We've got too little earth
and too much fire. We don't know who we are.
We're lost in the forest, and black stars
move lazily above us as if
they were only our dream.

But still, the second angel mumbled shyly,
there's always a little joy, and even beauty
lies close at hand, beneath the bark
of every hour, in the quiet heart of concentration,
and another person hides in each of us—
universal, strong, invincible.
Wild roses sometimes hold the scent
of childhood, and on holidays young girls
go out walking just as they always have,
and there's something timeless
in the way they wind their scarves.
Memory lives in the ocean, in galloping blood,
in black, burnt stones, in poems,
and in every quiet conversation.
The world is the same as it always was,
full of shadows and anticipation.

He would have gone on talking, but the crowd
was growing larger and waves
of mute rage spread
until at last the envoys rose lightly
into the air, whence, growing distant,

they gently repeated: peace be unto you,
peace to the living, the dead, the unborn.
The third angel alone said nothing,
for that was the angel of long silence.

FROM MEMORY

The narrow street rears up from memory—
let it be this poem's larynx—
and the thick gray smoke above the coking plant,
casting sparks into the sky like a volcano,
repaying its debt to the stars.

My street: two proud old maids
with narrow lips—they'd survived Siberia
and Stalin; a young actor, craving fame,
and Professor G., who'd lost an arm in the Uprising
and wore his empty shirtsleeve like a sail.

I don't know anything yet, nothing's happened,
not counting the war or the massacre of Jews.
In winter gray snow lurks on rooftops,
alert as an Indian, dreading spring.
Vacation comes, a peeled orange.

A greedy priest gulps Gospels
in the crimson, Neo-Gothic church;
oh, heart of hearts, Christ's wounded breast.
Thank God for cream puffs after Mass
to help erase your Latin tortures.

In the barracks new recruits are training,
one of my friends plays the trumpet
like Miles Davis, only better.
Young ladies promenade
in wide starched skirts.

The ugly earth, gashed by flat
black rivers, scarred
like a German student's cheek,
held still all day; at night
it crooned in two languages,

and we also lived in two idioms,
in the cramped jargon of the commonplace, of envy,
and in the language of a great dream.
At noon the clouds' eye gently
opened, the eye of tears and light.

That summer was so hot and muggy . . .
The white sky hung above me like a circus tent.
I talked to myself, wrote letters,
dialed interminable numbers.
It was so stifling that ink
dried up in fountain pens. Hawks swooned.
I even sent a telegram, accepted
with a start by the dozing post office.
Drunken wasps reeled above the table,
sugar cubes burst in black coffee.
I wandered through the town and turned
slightly invisible, out of habit,
from despair. I talked to myself.
An airport, a train station, a church
shot up at the end of every street.
Travelers spoke of fires and omens.
I looked for you everywhere, everywhere.
Shutters were locked, borders sealed,
only clouds stole westward.
It was so hot, the lead dripped
from stained-glass windows.

CHINESE POEM

I read a Chinese poem
written a thousand years ago.
The author talks about the rain
that fell all night
on the bamboo roof of his boat
and the peace that finally
settled in his heart.
Is it just coincidence
that it's November again, with fog
and a leaden twilight?
Is it just chance
that someone else is living?
Poets attach great importance
to prizes and success
but autumn after autumn
tears leaves from the proud trees
and if anything remains
it's only the soft murmur of the rain
in poems
neither happy nor sad.
Only purity can't be seen,
and evening, when both light and shadow
forget us for a moment,
busily shuffling mysteries.

HOLY SATURDAY IN PARIS

But maybe it's just
the feast day of spring rain:
boats cruise the gutters
with sails made of yesterday's paper,
otherwise known as *Le Monde*.
The butchers are about to rub their eyes,
and the city will awaken, sad and sated.
Someone once saw the earth split open
and swallow up a bit of future.
Luckily the rip was insignificant
and may still be stitched.
Some birds began to stammer.
Let's go someplace else, you say,
where monks sing
their songs poured from lead.
Alas, in the Arab quarter
a cloud, two-headed like the tsarist eagle,
bars the road.
And two-headed doubts,
slim as antelopes,
barricade the damp street.
Lord, why did you die?

ON SWIMMING

The rivers of this country are sweet
as a troubadour's song,
the heavy sun wanders westward
on yellow circus wagons.
Little village churches
hold a fabric of silence so fine
and old that even a breath
could tear it.
I love to swim in the sea, which keeps
talking to itself
in the monotone of a vagabond
who no longer recalls
exactly how long he's been on the road.
Swimming is like prayer:
palms join and part,
join and part,
almost without end.

SISTERS OF MERCY

That was childhood, which won't come back—
berries so black the night was envious;
slim poplars rose above the narrow river
like sisters of mercy and weren't afraid of strangers.
From the balcony I could see a little street and two trees,
but I was also the emperor and listened blissfully
as my countless armies roared
and the captured Turkish banners fluttered.

I liked the taste of grass between my teeth,
the bitter maple leaves, the sour sweetness
of June's first strawberry in my mouth.
Sunday morning Mother made real coffee,
in church the old priest waged war on pride.
My heart hurt whenever I saw someone poor.
Blue and yellow countries lived inside the atlas;
big nations swallowed up little ones, but on stamps

you just saw resting eagles, zebras,
giraffes, and tiny tomtits with their breathless grace.
On the dark shop's dusty shelves
jars of sticky candies towered.
Scarlet moths flew out when they were opened.
I was a Boy Scout and got to know loneliness
in the woods when dusk fell, the owl cried,
and the oak boughs creaked alarmingly.

I read stories about knights, Russian folktales,
and Sienkiewicz's unending trilogy.
My father built me a miniature mill,
which spun swiftly in the mountain stream.
My bike outran the panting locomotive,
August heat melted the gray city like ice cream.
Berries so black . . . bitter maple leaves . . .
That was childhood. Blood and feast days.

HOUSTON, 6 P.M.

Europe already sleeps beneath a coarse plaid of borders
and ancient hatreds: France nestled
up to Germany, Bosnia in Serbia's arms,
lonely Sicily in azure seas.

It's early evening here, the lamp is lit
and the dark sun swiftly fades.
I'm alone, I read a little, think a little,
listen to a little music.

I'm where there's friendship,
but no friends, where enchantment
grows without magic,
where the dead laugh.

I'm alone because Europe is sleeping. My love
sleeps in a tall house on the outskirts of Paris.
In Krakow and Paris my friends
wade in the same river of oblivion.

I read and think; in one poem
I found the phrase "There are blows so terrible . . .
Don't ask!" I don't. A helicopter
breaks the evening quiet.

Poetry calls us to a higher life,
but what's low is just as eloquent,
more plangent than Indo-European,
stronger than my books and records.

There are no nightingales or blackbirds here
with their sad, sweet cantilenas,
only the mockingbird who imitates
and mimics every living voice.

Poetry summons us to life, to courage
in the face of the growing shadow.
Can you gaze calmly at the Earth
like the perfect astronaut?

Out of harmless indolence, the Greece of books,
and the Jerusalem of memory there suddenly appears
the island of a poem, unpeopled;
some new Cook will discover it one day.

Europe is already sleeping. Night's animals,
mournful and rapacious,
move in for the kill.
Soon America will be sleeping, too.

I WALKED THROUGH THE MEDIEVAL TOWN

I walked through the medieval town
in the evening or at dawn,
I was very young or rather old.
I didn't have a watch
or a calendar, only my stubborn blood
measured the endless expanse.
I could begin life, mine
or not mine, over,
everything seemed easy,
apartment windows were partway open,
other fates ajar.
It was spring or early summer,
warm walls,
air soft as an orange rind;
I was very young or rather old,
I could choose, I could live.

INDEX OF TITLES